HELLO SAINTS!

HELLO SAINTS!

Michael Myers
Jane Casserly Myers

ORANGE *frazer* PRESS
Wilmington, Ohio

ISBN 978-1949248-463

Published for the copyright holder by:
Orange Frazer Press
37½ West Main St.
P.O. Box 214
Wilmington, OH 45177

For price and shipping information, call: 937.382.3196
Or visit: www.orangefrazer.com or
hellosaints.com

Book and cover design by:
Orange Frazer Press with Catie South

This project was funded by Xavier University in Cincinnati, Ohio

Library of Congress Control Number: 2021913109

First Printing

*This book is a work of love and is dedicated to all those
who identify as LGBTQ+ among the student bodies, alumni,
faculties, staff, religious, and parish members whom Fr. B served.*

Acknowledgments

We express our heartfelt gratitude to the following colleagues and friends ...

Mike Graham, S.J., Xavier University president, 2001-2021, whose wisdom about the value of this work to honor the life and legacy of his mentor and companion, Al Bischoff, S.J., brought it to publication.

Brian Maley, Director, Alumni Relations/Executive Director, Athletic Development, Alumni Relations/Annual Fund, for his enthusiasm about getting this book into the hands of Xavier alumni.

Michael Marrero, partner, intellectual property, Ulmer & Berne LLP, for early encouragement of this project.

Rich Sofranko, for providing a number of his own photographs of Fr. B over the years, and for investing time in enhancing the quality of others we had collected. We are very grateful for his professional contribution. See more of Rich's beautiful work at *www.richsofranko.com.*

Members of the *Xavier University community* who provided particular photographs, including *Greg Rust,* retired Xavier photographer; *Anne Ryckbost,* University Archives & Special Collections Librarian; *J.P. Macura,* alumni athlete; *Roberta Whitely,* Coordinator of Liturgy and Music, Dorothy Day Center for Faith and Justice.

Each of those who provided personal testimonies (they are identified with their stories throughout the book) whose lives have been significantly changed by their encounters with Fr. B. Each of their heartfelt witness accounts has helped us to tell the story.

Ed Schmidt, S.J., former Senior Editor of America, the Jesuit Review; and currently Jesuit Scholar at the Center for Mission and Identity, XU, and Assisting Priest, Bellarmine Chapel; for hours of methodical and detailed proofreading.

Mary Anne Reese, for several photographs from her personal collection; and, as an accomplished writer herself, for her encouragement as she reviewed our manuscript.

Eric Sundrup, S.J., pastor of Bellarmine Chapel, who enthusiastically supported our writing and kept impatiently asking when the book would be ready so we could plan a book-signing with Al at the Chapel.

Dan and Debbie Cox, long-time Xavier friends, who believe in the book as a source of inspiration and spiritual nourishment even to those who have not personally known Fr. B.

Bellarmine Men's Group, for their support over several years of Fr. B and Michael Myers as they came to freedom and grace, embracing their unique sexualities.

TABLE OF CONTENTS

Foreword

In the words of Fr. Albert Bischoff's good friend and colleague, Rabbi Abie Ingber ...

In a world of constant din and tumult, Fr. B enters it with gentleness and humility. His very presence is welcoming and comforting. He embraces each student, each Saint, with a face that completely listens—his ears are patient to hear what is said, his eyes respond with affection, his mouth speaks words of comfort. Who would not speak to him?

Not one person I have ever met thinks of themselves as a Saint, and so Fr. B's call of *"Hello Saint"* is shocking and celebratory at the same time. One can only wonder, "Perhaps I am ... " Invoking John Lennon, "If you dream by yourself, it's just a dream; but if two share the dream, it's a reality." Fr. B dreams of giving sainthood to everyone; I dream of giving love to everyone. We worked together to make it a reality for our campus.

Catholic in the best sense means universal and welcoming. He has welcomed me, a rabbi, among the legions of people whom he encounters at Xavier. To be welcomed by Fr. B, completely and unequivocally, is life-changing and life-giving.

Al Bischoff, S.J. with Abie Ingber, Executive Director, Center for Interfaith Community Engagement, 2008–19, Xavier University, Cincinnati, Ohio.
Courtesy of the University Archives and Special Collections, Xavier University Library, Cincinnati, Ohio

Preface

Fr. Mike Graham, S.J., (President of Xavier University for twenty years), when once asked about Fr. Albert Bischoff, said simply, "When I grow up, I want to be just like Fr. B."

Fr. Al Bischoff's life has spanned almost one hundred years. We propose that his life provides a special window on the holiness and growth of all God's people. There are many Saints among us, but this beloved man has touched many thousands of lives at Xavier University, at Augustana Lutheran College, and other places in Cincinnati and the Midwest. We celebrate him, and all of us, in this book as we rise to his acclamation that we heard many times, *"Hello Saints!"*

This is not a biography of an important or powerful person. It is the story of an unassuming, flawed, and broken man. Fr. B's childhood, like many of ours, was both joy and darkness. For some, extreme darkness can point the way to extreme light. He bravely rose above the darker and more confusing experiences of his childhood to bring presence, light, and joy into the simple interactions and daily relationships of his adult life and ministry. In these ways his story speaks to all of us.

Join us in a celebration of the legacy of Fr. B's humanity. Let's together reflect on his charisms so we can learn to replicate them among those whom God has given to us. To love consciously and on purpose is a good legacy.

Father Bischoff and Brother Darrell Burns, S.J., were having lunch in the dining hall one day. "B" recognized a student walking by: "Hi, John, I finally remember your name." John replied, "I'm glad you remember my name, Fr. B, but I would much rather hear you call me 'Saint'!" Thousands of students, staff, and parishioners agree with John. Over the years all have loved hearing that familiar salutation, "Hello Saint!"

What if you have this book in your hand but you never knew Fr. Bischoff? Maybe a friend gave it to you as a gift or recommended it to you. Will it be worth taking time to read?

When you hear these stories, you will be reminded of others in your life who have touched you in a similar way. We can only encourage you to trust that there is something here that will hold up a mirror for you to enjoy a whole new image, perhaps a whole new identity, of who you are in Christ.

Think of this book as a witness and a testimony that people can believe in and live out. It may allow you to remember, celebrate, and learn again the impact and consolation from a special presence in your life. At the same time may it touch you and raise up gratitude for all your loving mentors, family, and friends. We are writing to help people give words to their experiences of Fr. B. It is our privilege to be uniquely equipped to do this from fifty years as his colleagues in ministry and his intimate friends. There are many others who also count themselves as his friends. We feel blessed because he loves and respects us all.

The long months of writing this book have been a creative process both for us and for Fr. B. We wrote while he prayed many hours before the tabernacle. We prayed a lot, too, and kept writing. Time

Mike Graham, S.J. presiding with Al Bischoff, S.J., at Xavier University Blessing of the Graduates, May, 2020.
Courtesy of Roberta Whitely

and love have led us into a companionship that has produced this book and a deeper lasting friendship. He tells us that we have captured his life and legacy, and that both have become clearer to him. For that we are already grateful.

The process has uncovered and evoked grace and freedom for "B." (Note that in these pages we and others refer to him as "Fr. B," just "B," "Al," or more formally "Father Bischoff"; and even his childhood and family nickname "Bud.") B has always seen himself as "a broken vessel" used by God for good. He sees how the slow work of God has healed him over his lifetime, and that God has used his gift of presence for others. Now, with humility and gratitude, he can celebrate great consolation along with us the readers. In his prayer and retreat in June 2018, he confidently discerned that God, indeed, wanted this book to be published so that it could do some good. May it awaken the joy of the Good News and the power of love that sets us free.

And, if you don't mind, this is also meant to be a tool of reflection *for you as it has been for us.* (Note, too, that in these pages we do use first-person pronouns at times for ourselves or for questions you might ask yourself.) Fr. B wants you to think more about your own journey than about his! Right now, hear in his voice, *"Hello Saints!"* That would delight him. It has always been his desire to touch us with the startling Good News of God's love. B also wants us to remember that laughter, like singing, doubles our openness to the Holy Spirit. So we hope you laugh, Saints!

And we know that for those who love God, all things work together for good; according to God's purpose we are called to be Saints.
(Rom. 8: 28)

—*Michael and Jane Myers*

Introduction

Early in his papacy, Pope Francis wrote this first paragraph to begin his inspiring apostolic exhortation on the call to holiness:

"Rejoice and be glad!" (Mt. 5: 12), Jesus tells those persecuted or humiliated for his sake. The Lord asks everything of us, and in return he offers us true life, the happiness for which we were created. He wants us to be Saints and not to settle for a bland and mediocre existence. The call to holiness is present in various ways from the very first pages of the Bible. We see it expressed in the Lord's words to Abraham: "Walk before me and be blameless." (Gen. 17: 11) [1]

Gaudete et Exsultate (Rejoice and be Glad)

In the last decade, we have witnessed beatifications and canonizations of St. Mother Teresa of Calcutta, of St. John Paul II, and of St. John XXIII, animator of the Vatican Council, and also of martyred Oscar Romero from El Salvador. U.S.-born priest Stanley Rother was declared a martyr of the church by Pope Francis on December 1, 2016, following his murder in Guatemala in 1981 in his rectory. This ordinary man who served with extraordinary faithfulness was beatified on September 23, 2018, in Oklahoma City, where he was born.

When Pope Francis addressed the joint U.S. House and Senate in September 2015, he named and celebrated for our inspiration four great Americans: Abraham Lincoln, Martin Luther King, Jr., Dorothy Day, and Thomas Merton. With the naming of these modern saints, it has become easier to imagine that saints are all around us. Even with flaws and deficiencies, we know we are members of the Communion of Saints as we pray in our Creed. We can be confident that our faithful departed family members are in heaven.

"Hello Saints!" Yes, you! Yes, me! Yes, your family members. Yes, your friends from high school and your roommates from college. Yes, your neighbors next door. Yes, the homeless and refugees. Yes, members all across the political spectrum. Yes, people of all genders and lifestyles, and varieties of human experience. Yes, people of all religions and spiritualities. Yes, the unborn and the dying. Yes, we repeat, *Hello Saints!*

Fr. B wants us to bless and claim every person we meet every day. This is the Gospel truth!

Every person has an immortal soul. All Christians agree, and many of the world's religions teach the doctrine of Imago Dei. Every one of us is made in the image and likeness of God. This is not just poetry. It has been declared as the definition of the very essence of who we are. The Father, Son and Holy Spirit are firmly planted within us and are lifting all of us into the divine life as Jesus was lifted up into the risen Christ. He continues to rise even out of the dead parts of us. Christ is inextricably blended with all of our human DNA, and the DNA of all creation. The whole universe groans in labor and sings with joy as we all ultimately approach our life's fulfillment to be joined in the Universal Christ.

Opportunities were given to Fr. B through ordination and his roles as high school teacher, associate pastor, confessor, spiritual director, and campus minister at Augustana Lutheran College and Xavier University. He had an advantage to enter the lives of young adults, faculty, and staff, lifelong single men and women, couples, LGBTQ persons, growing families of all types and ages, and aging and dying parishioners. You probably already know this. You are probably among them.

This diverse and splendid reign of God that we have just described seems impossible, but it's already here! This kingdom is not of this world, and yet it can be discerned among us, between us, and within us every moment of every day. When we see a dolphin surface at the beach, when we delight in monarchs fluttering through our yards, when children chase lightning bugs at dusk on a summer night, when one gives bread to the hungry and provides shelter for the homeless, when refugees are welcomed with dignity, we get a glimpse!

Christ surfaces for a moment in our senses. Our hearts grow lighter for an instant before returning to our default mode that normalizes everything. But always around the corner there will be a wedding or a rainbow or a magnificent artistic creation, a performance, or a child's drawing on a refrigerator. Always there will be kindness and heroism and courage and exquisite vulnerability.

Saints are everywhere. The Christ mystery is in every face, every pleading voice or hand, every giving smile. "Hello Saints" is a gift that belongs to everyone. It is our inheritance already given to us.

When Fr. B began teaching at Elder High School many years ago, he was booed! A chorus of "He went to St. X!" hissed around the room! But in his own inimitable manner, Fr. B won over those students. He's been winning over groups and individuals one after another ever since. During his seventy years of ordained Catholic priesthood, it has been not so much the Roman collar that impresses people. Nor is it the fact that he is a Jesuit. What impresses people is a very specific kind of humility. He is genuinely in awe of every person he meets! The selfless wonder and delight in his eyes has had the effect of celebrating the Light inside us.

If you have met him you have known this. But it is easy to take it for granted. He has worked his magic on groups of athletes, ROTC members, faculty, and, perhaps most especially, hard-working staff. Fr. B has a special love for the often-invisible workers who keep Xavier and other institutions looking good and growing. In fact, it was always his wish that, when he died, his casket be carried by several of the XU Physical Plant staff.

Anyone remember the late '60s when Xavier still had a football team? A bunch of them did something stupid that was against university policy. The consequence was that the whole team would be punished. They came to Fr. B asking if he would take them on a retreat as an alternative to the "punishment" the university wanted to impose on them. He said yes, and it turned out to be life changing! Countless athletes and their teams have long felt Fr. B's love and blessing.

Around 1973, for unrelated reasons, the university decided to drop the football team. Fr. B felt the pain of the players and the fans for whom it was an enormous loss. In solidarity with them he decided to begin fasting from lunch every day, putting the money aside. After several months of fasting and prayer he was inspired with an idea. Fr. B hosted a dinner for all the football players as a way of thanking them. He valued their contribution to the university and honored them for their humility at losing something that was so important to them. Like exceptional moments in our lives, this was a feast where these Saints knew they were appreciated, loved, and respected for their sacrifice.

Fr. B's ministry sanctified us, not by heavy intellectual or moral teaching but because he celebrated the goodness that is our true selves. He absolutely demonstrated that "love conquers all" and believed that the reign of God was the daily lived experience of those in true community.

See, here's the thing ... Our life as modern Americans is dominated by hundreds of transactions every day. We pay this for that. We text, we email and we respond. We make appointments and plan for events. Our day is defined by the bits of information and exchanges that have become the norm for our busy lives.

A university is a microcosm of this culture with students and faculty rushing to and from classes. But even with plenty on his schedule, Al was not focused on these kinds of transactions. He chose to be focused on relationships. The "next thing" never had his attention more than the person right in front of him. In fact, his chronic anxiety about institutions, authority, products, and performance drove him to find sanctuary in the sacred "now." He did not live for success, even though he liked to look good. He lived for the precious moments with you and me. This is his rare quality and gift, and the reason why we wrote and you are reading this book.

Isn't that how many of us remember him? Whether it was a few minutes on campus, in the cafeteria, or in the chapel, it was a feast of love with Fr. B and his Saints—all of us! He often added to his greeting, "What a joy to hear your voice!" or simply, "What a joy!" We all knew that's just how he felt.

HELLO SAINTS!

CHAPTER 1

Mr. Bojangles

As I (Rino Angelini) reflect on this opportunity to give witness to the brilliant ministry of Fr. Al Bischoff, it becomes clear to me that I cannot do so without summoning moments from my own life as a liturgical musician. Looking back, my path is so indelibly intertwined with his that it is difficult at times to separate them. Our two stories are bound to the times in which they occurred, so in some ways, the following offering provides a small window into those formative years that we shared as well as our overlapping stories.

I don't normally quote John Denver. In fact, I can't remember the last time I sang one of his songs. Well, yes I can. It was in my mom's hometown of Pacentro, Italy, and I was asked by my nephew, Luca, to play "Country Road." To my astonishment, he and his three twenty-something buddies started belting out every word in English and I was accompanying them on the guitar! Their singing was full-throated and proud! It was such fun!

That said, one of the lines of a Denver song that has always touched me is one that he directed to his wife: "Well, it's goodbye again ... sorry to be leaving you ... I just have to go ... it's anyone who'll listen to me sing."

It's a bittersweet sentiment but the part that I always identified with was the part about anyone who would listen to me sing. It takes one to know one, John Deutschendorf!

When what you do is sing, what you crave is someone to listen.

Fr. Al Bischoff, the pre-eminent shaper of souls, spiritual director extraordinaire, miracle-in-my-life and friend, gave that gift to me, and set me on the path for my life! In a way, he took me on as his personal troubadour. Guided by his belief in me, my career as a cantor and music minister began at Bellarmine chapel at Xavier University when I was in the seminary in Cincinnati. The pinnacle was the weekly 7:30 p.m. Mass on Sunday night where Fr. B filled the chapel, but it was also the weddings, funerals, home masses (remember those?) and more that gave me a musical platform that would be the envy of anyone who did what I did. While I was pursuing the standard classical Latin, Greek, French languages, English literature, philosophy and theology training at the seminary, B taught me culture, fine dining, friendship, prayer, preaching and storytelling. Or, should I say story *listening*. I was not much of a raconteur at that time, an introvert who loved to sing ever since the nuns bade me, a junior high student, teach songs to the younger classes at St. Charles Parish in Boardman, Ohio.

B enriched me and stretched me, and he formed me as a cantor. I was the son of immigrants, and he expanded my sense of other sensibilities. He was the yin to my yang. I came to see my role as cantor, music minister, choir director, liturgist and 'animator of the congregation' as a half-circle and B became for me the ideal template of the other half-circle as leader of prayer, preacher and homilist, and inspiration as presider. He served as the model for priests I hoped to work with in what would become my forty-year career in music ministry, a span during which his example was occasionally met, but never exceeded.

I didn't know all of this at the time, but it has become crystal clear in the rearview mirror. During the heady days following the Second Vatican Council, we who were blessed to have learned some of the best of the music of the Mass of the Roman Rite in Latin from the Liber Usualis, were now immersed in the Liturgy in our own tongue! For some priests, turning around to face the people during the mass catapulted them into a quasi-state of shock, deer in headlights. Others, however, were animated by the change, and B was most definitely up to the task, but in a gentle and humble manner.

Understandably, the weak link in my curve of the half-circle consisted of our first attempts at liturgical music. We went through a period of infancy and reproduced a childish—hopefully, some were at least child-like—repertory. I am still in awe of the patience that our professors and teachers maintained in allowing us to make our own mistakes, however sincerely and passionately delivered. By the time we reached the era of that 7:30 Mass at Bellarmine chapel, a healthy, mature repertoire was not fully formed, but at least our early, immature attempts had been discarded, and we began to borrow and supplement from our developing secular folk tradition.

B summoned an admirable degree of trust in those creative transitional times, and in so doing, he gave me the artistic freedom that allowed me to use the musical and poetic expressions of our early days of renewal to form a necessary bridge to that time when a deeper musical expression of our faith would nourish us in song. In this liminal time, we leaned into expressions of the contemporary music lexicon such as "Get Together," "Day is Done," "Blowing in the Wind" or "Pilgrimage."

Dear God, we have come to your table once again,
As weary and dark as the night.

We long to consume all the beauty of your love,

And to drink of your morning light.

For doubt drove us down as we walked along the road

And a rein of indifference held us back

But the maps of the mysteries weren't noticed by the blind

When fear turned the daylight black.

And many fell down as we walked along the way

For the world mixes truth with its lies

And some of us were beaten till we couldn't understand

That the light of the world is in your eyes!

We come now, we come to this place upon the road

Where the hearts of the dead are reborn

And the poverty of men sees your treasure once again

A diamond in a crown of thorns.

[from Michigan composer, Bob Franke]

Ed Gutfreund's "Your People of Faith" was a staple of our gatherings in those days. We borrowed "Shalom" from our Jewish family in faith and such pieces as "Turn, Turn, Turn," songs of our age that reflected our search for meaning and became expressions of our developing faith.

"Fair seed time had my soul!" B was a mentor like no other—and I was blessed with many formative professors, including the church historian Thomas Bokenkotter, scripture scholar Eugene Maly, English literature professor par excellence Thomas Savage, and Daniel E. Pilarczyk, Greek teacher, rector, and honest debater of all things conservative. But B was our pied piper, open and inquiring, joyful in his faith, honest in his doubt and authoritative in his values.

The way that B prayed was always an inspiration, the way that he broke the bread illuminating. Once, his prayerfulness in proclaiming the words of institution as he broke the large host emboldened me in my naiveté to offer as a post-communion reflection, Leonard Cohen's "Suzanne":

... But he himself was broken,

Long before the sky would open,

Forsaken, almost human,

He sinks beneath your wisdom like a stone.

And you want to travel with him,

And you want to travel blind,

And you think that you can trust him,

For he's touched your perfect body with his mind.

After all, no one embodied or emulated better than B the truth that poetry and narrative offer the best language of faith.

We shared together many an intimate learning experience. I'll never forget a time when we went to celebrate Mass with young women living in a nuns' residence for unwed mothers. After Mass, I was leading a sing-along with the women, and was asked to sing "Yesterday" by the Beatles. I can only imagine what went through B's mind as he witnessed the clumsy moment when a clueless seminarian and a circle of confined women sat together, singing the line "Yesterday, love was such an easy game to play, now I need a place to hide away." There was a deafening silence, and then—to my great relief—laughter, all around.

These were the kinds of moments we shared, emblematic of the times, marked often by the improvisation that was always an unspoken modus operandi between us, and a signal of his faith in me. These were the kinds of steadying moments that Fr. B provided me weekly and monthly for sharing my developing musical gifts and sensibilities. He modeled for me those elements of homilist and leader of prayer that I strived to develop and emulate.

When I first met Fr. Bischoff in 1968, I was a young seminarian and he had been assigned as our spiritual director. He was definitely like no other priest there! He taught an elective class on cinema, introducing us to films such as *On the Waterfront*. I had already been smitten by Leonard Bernstein's *West Side Story*, but now to have B peel back the layers of meaning in an Elia Kazan film starring Marlon Brando was an epiphany that informed me in ways I could not have imagined. Among these memorable experiences was the time when, after viewing *Zorba the Greek*, a few of us went back to B's room and attempted to imitate the dance performed by Alan Bates and Anthony Quinn in the movie! B, a great aficionado of film and musicals, OF COURSE had the soundtrack, which accompanied us, courtesy of his well-loved record player. He provided us such exquisite opportunities for fun in a setting that could be, well, rather stern.

He so enjoyed laughter and lightness, and we craved it not only against the backdrop of the seminary itself but also the context of the moment—the Vietnam War, the violence of the early Civil Rights movement, the assassinations of our beloved leaders and role models. In his capacity as spiritual director to a bunch of very serious young men, he offered inspiration and understanding, but served it up with a healthy dose of silliness. His laugh was the one that I loved more than anything until I met my future spouse and fell in love with hers.

What a listener he was! B was the source of some of my most profound feelings, revelations and insights by sharing his deep love and respect for art and cinema, theatre and literature, scripture and poetry, and even jokes. Through these diverse channels he deepened my appreciation for the life of the Catholic Church. I think what he shared—and I make no claims about his intentions—was a healthy love/hate relationship with the church as institution. I can remember the homily of one of his esteemed colleagues, Fr. Savage, entitled "Up Against the Wall, Mother Church!" in which the author argued that any institution with 2,000 years of tradition will cling to ideas and practices that should have been tossed out long ago. But B taught me how to find some of the best elements of that tradition—ancient and newly discovered.

As a quite recent example of this, I would like to allude to the last homily (paraphased below) that I heard from B, as he addressed the 2020 graduating class of Xavier University (one of my Alma Maters, as the seminary shared the staff of XU in offering its Masters in Philosophy), B was still brilliant in his 90s as he proclaimed timeless words from a life lesson in the Gospel of Christ:

> In times like these, Saints, doubt may haunt you. But as you come
> here Sunday after Sunday at the invitation to become Christ's
> body ... so that we can become his love in the world ... You will find
> in your life, as I have found in my own life, as we hear today in the
> gospel about Thomas, that Christ still walks through locked doors.
> (See Appendix F for the entire text of the homily.)

I am tempted to end by recounting the pantheon of remarkable heroes and mentors among whom I align Fr. Bischoff, but suffice it to say:

> I knew a man Bojangles and he'd dance for you ...

When out of the blue I sang a bit of Mr. Bojangles, a song Fr. B loved, at the end of B's final Mass at Bellarmine during that period, he stood up from his presider's chair during the refrain and did a five-second soft-shoe—to the memory of which and to the man who performed it, I say: Thank you, Fr. B! Thank you, B! Thank you, Saint! Thank God for you, Fr. B!

With love,
Rino Angelini
Musician and composer

CHAPTER 2
So Why ...

Listen to Fr. B's all-time favorite Scripture passage:

Because you are God's chosen ones, holy saints and beloved, clothe yourselves with heartfelt mercy, with kindness, humility, meekness and patience. Bear with one another; forgive whatever grievances you have against one another. Forgive as the Lord has forgiven you. Over all these virtues put on love, which binds the rest together and makes them perfect. Christ's peace must reign in your hearts, since as members of the one body you have been called to that peace. Dedicate yourselves to thankfulness. Let the word of Christ, rich as it is, dwell in you. In wisdom made perfect, instruct and admonish one another. Sing gratefully to God from your hearts in psalms, hymns, and inspired songs. Whatever you do, whether in speech or in action, do it in the name of the Lord Jesus. Give thanks to God the Father through him. (Col. 3: 12–17)

On All Saints Day, Fr. B began his preaching by saying, "For me, one of the gifts every All Saints Day is receiving cards and emails from people I have known over many years, wishing me and themselves a Happy Feast Day!" They reflect on how hearing that name "Saint" impacted their lives when they were on campus, and how it has stayed with them all these years later.

> Am "I" a Saint?
> Why does Fr. B call me that?
> Why does it affect me so?
> And why has it affected so many people he called "Saints"?

It's unexpected and bold—a proclamation of the possibility that I will live forever with God. Most of us have been affirmed by parents, teachers, and mentors; but who has ever said to us, "I believe that you are a Saint and that you will live forever." In that one simple greeting Al Bischoff has been able to enlighten us as surely as any Zen master who awakened his student with a slap!

Fr. B is sincere. He is credible. He knows God. Therefore, if he calls me Saint maybe I am one. Yikes! So then I must ask myself, *"Am I really a Saint?"*

> If so, what does it mean?
> If it is right that he calls me a Saint, then
> what does that require of me?
> Is it just a happy thought?
> Does it echo inside of me?
> Does hearing it stir up anything? What?
> Do I dare to let it stir up more than just a smile?
> If I am a Saint, what now, what next?
> Does being called a Saint mean that I
> am for sure going to heaven?

Will I be raised from the dead some day with all the other Saints?

Can even ordinary people be living Saints?

Does it mean I have to be "good" all the time now?

What is the Communion of Saints?

How did his acclamation that I am a Saint move me forward

in life when I first heard it?

Do I want it to move me even now as I read this book?

Is it easier to hear "Hello Saints" when we are with others in a group? There is a subtle but important difference in the power of first hearing this acclamation with others. For many it feels quirky and amusing when hearing it for the first time. Then, when I hear "Saint" addressed just to me, am I more ready to hear it? Over time, it becomes a mantra that echoes and resonates and pursues us. It actually sounds even more true.

Maybe I should just forget what he said and resign myself to the practical concerns of my daily living. After all, I'm really busy. I have to go to work, do the wash, prepare dinner, to pay bills. What am I supposed to do with these questions when what I have to do just to survive in the present is so consuming? These questions are too big, and I have practical concerns that never end.

But the thing about Fr. B is, when he calls me "Saint," he requires no particular response. It isn't a test; it's an affirmation. There are no preconditions whether I am rich or poor, whether he sees me on campus or at Kroger's or in church or in prison, whether I am Catholic or not, whether I am a Muslim or a Jew, whether I am Black or Brown or White or another race, whether questioning everything or questioning nothing. When he says, "Hello Saints," it's done!

Like having water poured over us again it's like a new Baptism!

Fr. B is older, he's wiser, he's a priest, he's close to God. He must be right. *"Holy ####, I am a Saint!"*

Where do I go with all of this? What does it mean for my life? This little book may address some of this, but more importantly, we must each return to these questions on our own time and answer them for ourselves. Fr. B himself has always done this in his own struggle with accepting God's love. He believes in us. That's why he allowed us to write this book. Thank you for picking it up and letting him again call you "Saint."

CHAPTER 3

The Brief Story of Al Bischoff's Long Life

Albert John Bischoff was born on January 19, 1927, in Cincinnati, Ohio, to Margaret Mahlenkamp and Albert John Bischoff. He had one older sister, Ruth Catherine, born in 1924, who later married Tony Wesselman. Together Ruth and Tony adopted three children, Bob, Martha, and Mary Ruth.

During the first six years of his life he lived with his mother's parents behind Glenway Tire Shop. He attended Carson Kindergarten and tells the story of how one day while taking his nap lying on the newspaper on the floor, he accidentally tore the edge of it. His teacher, Miss Lemon, did not let him go out to play that day.

Fr. B was, and in some ways will always be, a Price Hill-Western Hills-Cincinnati boy. "Albert" was baptized at Resurrection Parish, where he spent his early childhood. He later celebrated his First Communion and Confirmation at St. Teresa's. During those years Albert and his classmates walked home for lunch. Along the walks, his precocious inner world stirred up questions like, "I wonder what hell would be like?"

On other days he looked forward to the beautiful tradition of the May crowning, when the children were encouraged to bring flowers from home to lay at the foot of the statue of Mary in the church courtyard. Even though his family had only a small garden, Albert always brought the biggest basket home from school, eager to fill it! His father worked the gas station and car repair shop at the corner of Glenway and Iliff, originally owned by Al's grandparents, Ed and Frances Mahlenkamp, who lived in a big house right behind it. Al's dad later confidently took over the business.

Al remembers that the new Glenway Park opened up in the woods near his house. In the fall they built campfires and roasted apples and marshmallows. There was something very sacred about those moments, as if sharing Holy Communion together. Another image of little Bud is whimsically skipping home from school while reciting, "The time has come, the Walrus said, to talk of many things: of shoes—and ships—and sealing wax—of cabbages and kings ... " from "The Walrus and the Carpenter" by Lewis Carroll. From the time he was six until a senior in high school, Al's family lived at 4624 Joanna Place in Price Hill.

In school "Albert" was known by his baptismal name, but at home he was affectionately called "Bud" by his parents and his sister. A popular name throughout Europe, his family surname means "bishop" in German.

When he was eight or nine years old, little Bud made several entries in his journal about an experience of being assaulted and violated by a group of young boys. He would later over many years return to these memories in therapy and in prayer, longing to be released from their destructive hold on him.

When Bud was ten, his father took their family that summer to Lake Wawasee, Indiana. Al clearly remembers during that trip going to see the film *Goodbye, Mr. Chips.* Afterward, his parents noticed that he was very quiet and thoughtful. "Buddy is something bothering you?" Bud confidently replied, "I am going to be a teacher!"

Since Al's father had only a sixth grade education, he would ask his son to entertain the family after dinner by reading his favorite sections of the newspaper. His mother was not typical of Price Hill mothers. She was more interested in politics than cooking or cleaning. She loved books and regularly took Bud to the library, instilling his love of books and learning. His mother's favorite book, which she read to Al as a child, was the classic *The Birds' Christmas Carol* by Kate Douglas Wiggin. Going to the theater together to enjoy plays and musicals was one of his favorite ways to spend time with her.

Politically active, his mother was actually a feminist, conscious of justice issues, who wrote to oppose the draft and World War I. She belonged both to a Catholic Women's Group and even to a non-Catholic group. Al remembers that when Dorothy Day came to Cincinnati his mother eagerly took him to hear her.

Fr. B's own family members had a very quiet home life. Feeling he was missing out, he longed for the piano music, singing, and laughter of large family gatherings. During high school he spent a lot of time at the home of his good friend, Bob Conway, and at the Janson family home. That's when he felt like a true romantic, imagining himself singing and dancing like Bing Crosby and Fred Astaire.

He recalls his high school days as some of the happiest in his life. While many of his childhood friends attended Elder, Al and his parents instead chose St. Xavier High School. That decision would significantly impact the trajectory of his life.

A favorite entertainment he enjoyed was riding the street car downtown to Fountain Square then walking to theaters to see special performances. In December of 1941 he went to see the Andrews Sisters perform. When he arrived home his mother told him the news that Japan had just bombed Pearl Harbor and that we were at war. Unaware of the consequences of this sober news, he responded by eagerly telling her about the show he had just seen and innocently singing the songs that were still playing in his head. "Don't sit under the apple tree with anyone else but me ... 'til I come marching home."

A. J. Bischoff

Class of 1945 photo hanging at St. Xavier High School.
Courtesy of Mary Anne Reese

He had a wonderful group of close friends, guys and girls, who enjoyed spending time together. They affectionately called him "Bisch." Among them was Lois Levy, at the time the love of his life. Her father was Jewish, and Al's father let him know he was not pleased with his son's choice. Later when he actually met Lois, Al's father quickly changed his opinion and encouraged Bud to pursue this beautiful girl.

Al knew in his heart that he was not called to marry Lois. When he finally disclosed this decision, he thought he would ease her disappointment by telling her whom he thought she should marry instead! Of course, she protested. But, guess what? Lois did end up marrying the young man Al had recommended, Bob Johannigman. They had a long and beautiful marriage, which was a great consolation to Al.

The summer of 1944, when he turned eighteen, his family moved to 448 Cincinnati-Louisville Pike (now Bridgetown Rd.) on an acre of land next door to a nursery.

He graduated from St. Xavier High School in 1945. During that summer he went to the Jesuit seminary in Milford. He had the first of many mystical experiences there. One he recalls is clearly seeing the statue of the Sacred Heart out through the window of the adoration chapel. His own heart prayed the prayer, "O Sacred Heart of Jesus, I implore that I might love you more and more." Then from his own heart came these words added to the prayer, "and that I might let you love me more and more!" Years later he reflected, "All of my most important spiritual decisions were made at Milford."

But he was unhappy there at Milford. He had left his wonderful high school friends behind and missed them greatly. He would walk in his long black cassock down to the Little Miami River. There he would see young couples having picnics on the other side. He would wave to them as a simple and guileless way of feeling included in their courtship. They would always wave back. This is a sweet and iconic memory for him. Even then he craved relationship and community. He later came to realize that during those days he was deepening his understanding of the mystery of the Incarnation, that God took on human flesh, and that actually our human flesh takes on the divinity of God! Within just two months, on August 14, 1945, he left Milford.

In September 1945, Japan surrendered, and Fr. B was immediately drafted. The Army physician who gave him his required physical examination decided on a 4-F deferment, saying, "You're one of those good people who is 'unfit for duty;' not suited for war." Even though he felt guilt and shame about not serving, with the support of his loving friends, he joined the many young men coming home from the war going to Xavier University. He began as a pre-med major but soon decided to pursue teaching instead, majoring in history with a minor in philosophy and English.

In 1948 he did his student teaching at Purcell High School and was so successful that Dr. McCoy, the dean of the Education Department at XU, encouraged him to go on for his master's degree. Al knew that he wanted to teach in public schools and that he would need higher education in addition to his experience teaching at a Catholic school.

Fr. B graduated from Xavier University in the class of 1949. In September he learned about an opening in a public school in Fayetteville, and he replaced several sisters teaching geography, math, and social studies. He was offered $2100 as his first salary, but when he arrived on the first day he was told that the school could afford to pay him only $2000. Among his duties that first year were teaching, advising the student newspaper, directing the school play, and being an umpire for the baseball team. His job with the baseball team lasted only one game. He was fired the next day since he knew nothing about baseball!

Fr. B was living very simply as a renter in a rooming house, and he went to St. Patrick's every day for Mass. He soon came to realize that he would never get married. That awareness, together with his chronic fear of going to hell, motivated a growing desire to serve. He began to wonder again if God could really use him as a priest, so he entered St. Mary's Seminary in September 1950. His favorite teachers there were Fr. Eugene Maly for Scripture and Fr. Carl Steinbicker in Church History, who spoke several years later at his ordination.

On May 26, 1956, Albert J. Bischoff was ordained a Catholic priest at St. Monica's Parish in Corryville. St. Peter in Chains Cathedral was undergoing renovation at the time. The celebration was a stunning moment in the life of his family. While his mother was disappointed to not have grandchildren, both she and his father were very proud that he had become a priest. He himself was deeply grateful to have found a life centered in relationship, service to God's people and community. He had found his true calling.

His first assignment was to St. Monica Parish, where he served for six years, 1956–1962, presiding and doing pastoral work while also being "teacher in residence" at Elder High School.

In 1962 he was appointed associate pastor of Resurrection Parish, returning to the church and community where he had been baptized thirty-five years earlier. He served there for six years until 1968.

For twelve years, from 1956 until 1968, Fr. B taught at Elder High School. Although he was anxious about teaching at Elder since he had not gone to high school there, he connected with the students and had "an absolutely wonderful experience." Since high school had been for him the happiest time in his life, he understood young people and had a genuine way of engaging them. He taught English for nine years and Religion for three, particularly enjoying teaching the new understandings and spirit emerging from Vatican II. For several of these years Fr. B was also chaplain of Fort Scott, the archdiocesan Catholic summer camp.

Butch Otting recalls this memory:

I was lucky enough to have B as my 3rd year English teacher in 1963. He was a challenging yet fair teacher and was interested in how the students related to the course material and also how it was reflected in current events. He would often pick a novel for reading and discussion in class. This particular year he had chosen Nathaniel Hawthorne's *The Scarlet Letter*. In each class he typically would pick one student at random to read a section and talk about its meaning and significance within the novel. One day, however, our English class decided to turn the tables on him. Looking ahead to the discussion for the day and prior to his arrival in class, one of the students dressed as Hester Prynne, complete with a wig, dress and a large red A, and hid in the classroom cupboard. After class began and the selection from the novel had been read, B started the discussion. Just then the student burst out of the closet shouting, "Reverend Dimmesdale, Reverend Dimmesdale!" and ran to B, jumped into his arms and embraced him. At first flustered, B soon regained his composure and replied, "Now Hester, it is okay to show your feelings, but please don't let this get back to the principal."

B's influence extended well beyond the classroom. He would be the first one to tell you that he was not athletic, and yet he often was the chaplain for school sports teams. He had a sympathetic ear always ready to listen to students and young adults. For me personally this was very true. I was fortunate to be offered scholarships to several different colleges. In talking with B, he helped me discern which would be the option that suited me best. In the end I chose Xavier, and it turned out to be the right place for me in so many ways. Along the way he also suggested a summer job as a counselor at Fort Scott Camps. He saw something in me of which I was not aware. He was a sounding board helping me to see possibilities and make good choices. Xavier and Fort Scott have had a tremendous influence on my life; I discovered more about who I was, what my gifts are, and have made lifelong friends in the process. I am but one example. Many, many more have had similar experiences with B.

Elder High School was not protected from the tension that was felt all over the country. He and the other priests on the faculty, including Fr. Ed Hussey and Fr. Malcolm Grad, were personally very troubled by these painful times.

In 1966, while at Resurrection parish, he and several Elder students started a contemporary folk Mass; up to 600 teens came every Sunday from all over the city to a church designed for only

450! He had to work it out with the police and fire department. The very talented musicians were seminarians, Rino Angelini, Joe Sandman, Lee Yeazell, Pete Heile, and Frank Evans. He always stressed over his homilies, wanting to be "real." "But then the Lord told me to just tell stories. That's what they needed to hear from me."

Frank Evans shares his memories of those days:

Where do you start to recall thoughts and memories of 52 years? I first met B at the Seminary. He was a teacher and took a room in Fenwick Hall. Several of us became fast friends and bonded quickly with him. He was a breath of fresh air in a world of archaic rules and regulations about to change with Vatican II.

As that year went on we met many friends of his. I remember Fr. Rudy, Fr. Buening, Fr. Hassellhoff and others, including Fr. Bob Hungling from Resurrection Parish where B had a 7:30 evening Mass and a group of us would sing. I was told it was the first guitar Mass in the city. I don't know that for sure but we enjoyed mingling with so many young people who packed the place to hear him preach. That was B's gift. He was able to send a message to all that whatever they are or have done, God forgives and loves them.

I'm sure many of you have some fantastic stories and great memories. Mine were borrowing his car to make a late night run to Arby's, spending the night in his room on the phone talking with girls he introduced us to, crying over a botched exam, dealing with some personal or family issue. We've all been there and heard we were still OK.

I first invited B to Massillon to my parent's home for a holiday. As the years went by B has married, buried, baptized and befriended everyone in my family. He became especially close to my brother, John, and my grandfather Bomp who lived on a farm in Harrison. B would often come to visit and the two of them would end up walking in the fields for hours.

I also was privileged to get close to B's family, sharing fun times sitting around their kitchen table devouring a bucket of KFC and listening to stories about "Bud" as only his mother could describe. Fond memories.

During this time, privately he felt guilty that there was so much loneliness in all his family members. He heard God telling him, "Albert, don't beat yourself up. I love you!"

In 1968 Archbishop Karl J. Alter assigned Fr. B to St. Gregory's Seminary to a position on the faculty in the high school division, to teach history and religion, to get to know the students, and to model the life of a priest for them. Dr. Vytautas Bieliauskas and the dean of students, Fr. Pat Raterman, were also recruiting him to come to XU ... Xavier won! So he left St. Gregory's after one year, in 1969.

After Al left the seminary he tried to understand what was really going on within himself. Still searching, at Xavier University in 1969 he was assigned to live with students in Kuhlman Hall, to teach Theology, and to be a "campus presence." This was the birth of campus ministry on Xavier's campus. Al committed himself to presiding at the 7:30 PM Sunday Mass, assisted by the same young talented musicians from Resurrection who had followed him to Xavier. In addition to the campus community, many young people from around the city were drawn to Christ through the experience of celebrating the Eucharist with Fr. B.

With the Vietnam War raging, Al's conscience, formed in part by his mother's sense of justice, moved him to burn his draft card during a Mass at the Armory at Xavier.

In 1974 Fr. B was given a new assignment and was appointed associate pastor at St. Margaret Mary in North College Hill. While serving there, he began fresh new pastoral initiatives including marriage ministry and baptism ministry. Inspired by his creative young Director of Religious Education, Mike Myers, together they inaugurated the first RCIA (Rite of Christian Initiation of Adults) in the archdiocese; and they suspended a wagon wheel from the sanctuary ceiling to hold the four candles of a beautiful Advent wreath. Even though he came to dearly love the people and the community, Fr. B longed for a deeper fellowship that would give him a depth of thinking, feeling, praying and sharing life. As he discerned and continued reflecting on his experience at Xavier, the call became clear. He decided to apply to the Jesuits and left the parish in 1979.

Waiting for an answer became torture, though, as he found himself increasingly each day wanting to be accepted. Finally, one night, on the eve of Epiphany, he went to the church to pray. "God, I just need to hear something from you." The very next day, on a Monday, a letter arrived inviting him into the Company of Jesus (the Jesuits).

On September 8, 1979, Al entered the Jesuits, moving to Berkeley, Michigan, to live and study in the novitiate. If you knew Fr. B, you knew of his longtime friendship with Leo Klein, S.J. It was Leo who, as his provincial, accepted him into the Jesuit community. In his role, Leo made a call to Archbishop Daniel Pilarczyk to inform him of this change in status of one of his diocesan priests. The archbishop's response was, "This news does not surprise me; in fact, it makes me very happy."

Here's a letter written on January 22, 1979, from a former student of Fr. B's at St. Gregory Seminary after hearing that Al joined the Jesuits:

Dear B,

You never told me that being a priest was so damned crazy!

Ever since I heard the news about you joining the Jesuits, I've been full of excitement and prayers for you. Every time I see those two letters (SJ) together I think of all the prayer and thought you must have been putting into this more important decision.

In my more whimsical moments, B, I consider writing to Pedro to make sure he knows that he's getting just about the best there is, but I don't know too many Spanish superlatives ... Honest, B, sometimes I think about the way I deal with people, or my spirituality, the way I celebrate liturgy—a *lot* about my Christianity and my priesthood—and I know it's there because of you.

I've been affected a lot along the way to where I am now (and where I'm going, for that matter) by teachers, preachers, etc., priestly and otherwise, and you really are one of the more prominent ones, B. I think one of the best lessons I learned from you at St. Greg's was how important it is to affirm people. I never remember a single occasion, walking away from an encounter with you, that I didn't feed my self-worth and importance as a person to a greater extent. It was a hell of a lesson, B, and I still remember it.

Much love and prayers,
John

That same year, 1979, Al buried his father just a couple of days before Christmas.

In the fall of 1980, Fr. B began studying at the Jesuit School of Theology in Chicago. The next few years would include the continuation of a modified formation program which became a welcome emancipation away from Cincinnati for a while. On September 8, 1981, he took his first temporary vows in the chapel at the Schott Building on Xavier's campus.

In 1981 he was assigned to St. Ignatius Parish as associate pastor. This transition became more challenging than anticipated, and he suffered a nervous breakdown. He left the parish after just one year. While still at St. Ignatius in 1982, Fr. B was able to give a retreat for seminarians of the Precious Blood Community at St. Joseph's in Rensselaer, Indiana. Years later he heard from several of the men how significant the retreat had been for them. They said it was not what he had said, but what he had showed them, what he represented, that had stayed with them.

Realizing that Al needed a place to recover, in 1983 Leo Klein arranged for him to return to Milford for an extended time of rest and prayer.

From there Al moved to Augustana Lutheran College in the "Quad Cities" on the Mississippi River in Rock Island, Illinois, where he lived in a house of prayer. He formed a group of six women and six men, an ecumenical group named "the Apostles," who met weekly for two years, deepening their faith as they committed themselves to living as disciples on campus. Routinely, a large group of the student body would attend Mass. Catholic students whose faith had been weak found it strengthened; some were led to the sacrament of confirmation. A number of non-Catholic students were inspired to come into full communion with the Catholic Church, transformed by the Holy

Spirit through the charism of Fr. B. Most of the football players during those years were Catholic. It is legend that Fr. B was part of the secret to four consecutive national championships for Augie! Not one more since he left!

Here's a letter from "one of those saints" at Augie dated September 29, 1997:

I don't know if you remember me, but I was one of the saints whom you bailed out of trouble. I attended Augie from the fall of 1986 to 1990. I was a BOS and pledged with the likes of S. and P. I doubt that I would have made much of an impression, but for an incident in which I was involved that dealt with a Poobah/COG homecoming float and a fire.

I am certain that I would have been expelled had you not interceded on my behalf with the school administration. What was most touching about what you did for me was that I didn't come to you. You reached out to me. My penalty was still stiff, and deservedly so, but thanks to you I remained in school and graduated on time.

I think that I will always be in your debt. I don't know how things would have turned out if you hadn't been there for me, but I can certainly think of some scenarios that involve words like expulsion and felony-arson. I went to law school after Augie and I am now an attorney for a chemical company in Tennessee with a concentration in environmental laws and regulations.

I just wanted to drop you a line to let you know how much you meant to all of us at Augustana. In dealing with

some of us, especially the BOS fraternity, you probably
felt more like Father Flanagan at Boystown than the
Augustana College Chaplain. Your sincere, unconditional
affection for us was touching. You are the true saint!

Kindest regards,
Mike

In 1983 Fr. B's mother was getting close to death, so he came
home to Cincinnati on the Wednesday before Holy Thursday and
stayed through Easter Sunday. On Easter Monday he returned to Augustana and received a call when he arrived that his mother had died
the night before on Easter.

In 1988 Fr. B was again invited to return to XU. He moved into the
residence hall, this time into Husman, as part of the campus ministry
team. That year, at the age of 62, Al began seeing Dr. Richard Brush a
psychiatrist, in Cincinnati. He saw him three times a week for three
years, then less often.

When Fr. B left Augustana in 1988 many felt a great loss, including Dorothy Parklander, who with her husband lived right across the
street from his residence there. In a letter she wrote to him on September 12, 1989, she said, "Dear Albert, it was a particular joy to find
a note from you at the beginning of this school year. You cannot imagine how much I miss you, your visits to me and the wonderful sense
of your living across the street where I could feel my own world held,
framed, bonded with the sense of your understanding and love and
compassion. The emptiness now is enormous, simply because you being there made a difference, immediate and real."

On December 2, 1991, Fr. Al Bischoff took his final vows of commitment into the Society of Jesus at Bellarmine Chapel.

From 1992 until 1998, Fr. B was assigned to Brebeuf Jesuit High School in Indianapolis as rector of six Jesuits. During these six years, he drove from Indiana once a month to see Dr. Brush until he returned to Cincinnati. (When Dr. Brush died in 2010, Al lost a beloved friend as much as a professional who had accompanied him on some dark paths that lead the way to much healing and peace.)

At Brebeuf he was sought out as spiritual director by the faculty and the local archbishop and ministered to a community of Carmelites who begged him to stay. Faculty and students regularly invited him into their classrooms for engaging discussions about faith. While there he also met many wonderful couples and families, among them John and Maryann Grogan, who have stayed in touch, whom he still visits, and who describe him this way:

Father Al and I parked next to each other in the Brebeuf Jesuit Preparatory School parking lot in Indianapolis in August, 1992. His burgundy sweatshirt stamped "Xavier Rugby" did not alert me that this was the beloved "Fr. Al Bischoff" the Brebeuf community was waiting for. Since Indianapolis was not a "rugby" town at that time I asked him if rugby was "real" at X? His smile and chuckle led to introductions and the start of decades of friendship. Dinner at the Grogan's followed as John and I welcomed Fr. Al for dining-room theology where we relished being called Saints.

Fr. Al's love of stage showed itself in an early homily where he had preached with the theme that the "gift was not the wrapping." At the end of his message Fr. Al ducked down behind the pulpit to reappear with ribbons and bows adorning his wonderful bald head. We all got the visual and remember the message forever.

Fr. Al has journeyed with us sharing our family life and enriching our ability to see the presence of God in what we do every day. He lives his life showing us that actions matter, and that there is joy in everything we experience. We are grateful to have a Saint among us whom we call family.
(Mary Ann)

When Father Al arrived at Brebeuf all three of our children, who had graduated from Brebeuf, were in college. Although Father Al did not know them in high school he soon forgave all their known and unknown sins and canonized them as Saints. Later after Father Al returned to Xavier University, my sister-in-law, who lived nearby, would attend Mass at Bellarmine Chapel with Father Al and recognize that some of his homilies' anonymous stories obviously came from our family. We were always relieved that there was a veil of confessional secrecy.

In the halls of Brebeuf or walking the campus of Xavier when we visited Father Al, it was obvious that all students were Saints and truly loved and respected this wonderful, gentle, caring, and thoughtful priest.
(John)

This letter, sent on January 30, 1998, from Mark Lubbers, describes the gift of Al's presence among the community there:

Dear Father Bischoff,

Given your native humility, I'm certain that you hate hearing how much we'll all miss you and how wonderful we think you are.

But, then again, you are as wise as you are humble, and you know that expressing these feelings is important for us. So, if you are finding it difficult to suffer the indignity of so much fawning, just remember you're doing it for us ... like so many other things you've done for us since you came to Brebeuf.

As always, God has a plan for every step we take (even when it's a step away from Him)! And when He sent you to us, it was to be a subtle miracle-worker. Your healing touch sustained us through Pat's death and the year following. In so many ways, you were the bearer of the grace to get many of us—especially Kate and Fred—through that year.

... which is to take nothing away from your leading "the saints" ever since in a gentle, sometimes direct, sometimes indirect, but always Christ-like way. Your presence at Brebeuf has been a history-changing tenure. We have come so far in the past six years and so much of that progress traces back to your subtle miracle working.

As our older daughter gets set to enter Brebeuf, I was looking forward to seeing you again with greater frequency. Now, alas, you are stolen away! You always have a home here. Come see us and, by all means, keep us in your prayers as you will be in ours.

Sincerely,
Mark

That same year, during his birthday month of January, he received another letter from his lifelong friend, Bob Conway:

Dear friend, Albert,

I am writing to wish you a Happy Birthday! 70 offers a glorious veranda from which to look back, to reflect on all the wonderful experiences. What a blessed diary of God's presence in your life ... The bitter cold of the past week has reminded me often of the days we shared together at XU. Somehow I recall the cold, snowy days and your generous care of your motley assortment of friends. What happy memories! You are still in my mind and heart, Bud ... I am carried along by these blessed memories of a dear friend who is and has been a very special blessing to me for almost all of my life.

I love you,
Bob

Bob sent another birthday letter the following January in 1999:

Albert, my old, dear friend, you never disappoint. What a remarkable feat. True to that unbelievable record is the grace and poise that you bring to the weddings of our children ... Thank you so much for your selfless devotion to our family that makes possible such stirring religious experiences that become, because of your special touch, spiritual experiences as well. We love to talk about it afterward and repeat the joy. Have a very special birthday, Bud, full of peace and joy and content knowing that you are indeed a very special saint of the Lord's. You are in the thoughts and prayers of all the Conway's. Ruth wants to thank you especially for the experience of a blessing-filled retreat.

Love and appreciation,

Bob

In 1998, his provincial and friend, Leo Klein, S.J., learned that Fr. B's sister Ruth was failing in health, so he invited Al to return to XU. He had served his six years as rector at Brebeuf, so it was a natural time for a new ministry assignment. Fr. B. again moved into Husman Hall, continuing to live with students as a member of the campus ministry team.

It was a difficult year, but he was glad to be back. This was a year he "learned more about how to really pray." During a conversation with his spiritual director, he realized, "I feel like Swiss cheese. I am full of holes." His spiritual director replied, "Those holes are the spaces where God can get in. And Swiss cheese is oh, so tasty. So be happy to be a common ham and cheese on rye, which everyone enjoys anyway." With this image came the deepening realization that Christ is incarnate in us and our suffering builds empathy for others. We need compassion to be authentic. When we commit to a life of mercy and justice, we reflect God's desire to set us free. It was that sense of freedom that was growing inside of Fr. B.

For the next twenty-one years Fr. B would be immersed in the life of students, staff, and faculty at Xavier. Living with the students in Husman Hall, he was closely and personally with them in their daily lives. And, as a presider at both Sunday and daily Eucharist at Bellarmine Chapel, he also became the familiar and loving Fr. B to the many children and adults who have been members of the Bellarmine parish family. It was his joy—and theirs—to celebrate countless baptisms, first Communions, confirmations, and marriages during these years. For the Bellarmine Chapel community he has been friend, personal "pastor," spiritual director, confessor, and beloved friend.

The 4:00 PM student Mass in the chapel had begun in 1969. Fr. B and Br. Darryl Burns continued to guide and train many students over the following years to plan, to perform liturgical ministries, and to join together in prayer and worship each Sunday afternoon. The 4:00 Mass became a calm and peaceful sanctuary of healing for the personal challenges and wounds the students brought to prayer, and encouragement and strength for the tough academic week ahead.

Al's beloved sister Ruth died on July 20, 2009, after living her last five years in a nursing home. Al and his sister always agreed on one thing, "Life is one long lesson in humility."

Fr. B's mother's birthday happened to be on the Fourth of July. During his summer retreat in 2014 he found himself trying to understand his relationship with her more deeply. That year on the Fourth he was inspired to realize that the rose revealed it all. The innocence and goodness of the rose, just as with his mother, was sometimes lost to Al even though he thought he knew and loved her. On that day he felt inspired to buy himself a rose and place it in a vase in his room to commemorate her life. Every week since then he continued the Saturday ritual of going to his favorite florist to buy one rose for himself and then a few more to sweetly give to women he met intentionally or spontaneously that day.

During Lent of 2016 Mike Myers invited Al to join him in offering a bimonthly men's group. Years later this group of men from Bellarmine Chapel still faithfully meets to support one another in vulnerability before God and each other.

Later in 2016 his last surviving cousin died at the age of ninety-one. (As of the writing of this book, he still has two nieces and a nephew for whom he cares very much.)

On January 19, 2017, Fr. B celebrated the milestone birthday of 90!! There were parties during the days leading up to it and for weeks following. It was a very big deal on Xavier's campus, in the Bellarmine Chapel community, and even throughout the City of Cincinnati. The local Channel 12 News team came to campus to interview him, then ran the story of his birthday four times on the news throughout the day.

In May 2019, after twenty years, Fr. B moved out of Husman Hall into the Jesuit residence on Xavier's campus at the age of 92. This very difficult discernment was the fruit of his own prayer together with his rector, Walter Deye, S.J. It was time. God clearly confirmed the decision with the gift of peace in Al's heart.

CHAPTER 4

His Extraordinary Gift of "Presence"

One afternoon Fr. B was sitting in the chapel in prayer. A young African American boy from the neighborhood shyly approached him. He said his mother had sent him to ask a minister what real love is:

"Are you a minister?"

"Yes, I guess I am."

"There's a girl in my class who says she loves me. She wants me to say that I love her, too. But love is forever, isn't it?"

"Well, it depends. God's love for us lasts forever."

"That's what I thought. This girl at school keeps trying to kiss me and tells me she loves me. I know that won't last forever. I want a love that will last forever."

"Good for you. Then your prayer will be answered."

Satisfied, the boy turned to other things.

"Are those candles yours?"

"No, they are not mine, but we could light one together."

Fr. B and the boy lit a candle and sat quietly together for a little while longer before the boy thanked him and left.

Note: In the spirit of this book as a tool for you, we encourage you to take a moment to light a candle and sit with Jesus the way Fr. B showed this young man.

Tom Kula knew Fr. B at Augustana College in Rock Island, Illinois back in the 80s. Here's how he recalls him:

> His honesty and appreciation for being in the moment with you is what I remember. Fr. B responds in a way that he accepts you no matter what and appreciates whatever struggles or joy you are experiencing. He exhibits the love Jesus has for us without preaching or talking down to us. Fr. B is one of the most significant persons in my life. What a huge loss it would have been for me if I had never gotten to know him. There are so many experiences that made him significant ... dinners at Augustana College, as teacher of my seminar class, as counselor and advisor when I was in trouble, as 2B cohort, as priest at my wedding and at the baptism of my son; as a good friend for over 32 years.

So, what is it about Fr. B's presence that touches us so personally? Can we describe this quality about him that draws so many of us?

Some have described it as childlike, available, nonjudgmental, humble, accepting, and safe. He touches and connects with our unconscious in a surprising, singular way. His very presence seems to create a space in which one can be oneself without pretending, without needing protection. His ego does not get in the way. In fact, he goes out of his way not to be an authority figure to others; consequently, he becomes a *genuine* authority in whom one can rest and trust. There is no real past in the encounter and no real projected future. The moment is especially freeing for you and for Fr. B. He may not remember your name, but there are no expectations, no strings attached other than enjoying the present.

One of the residence hall directors said of him, "No one had to teach Fr. B what to do or how to be with the students. He just knew it instinctively."

Here's another story: It was move-in day at Xavier University. New students were moving into Kuhlman Hall as they did each August. Fr. B was in the hallway around the corner and overhearing several guys bantering, "Can you believe we have to live with an old bald-headed priest on our hallway? What the #####? You gotta be #####in' kidding me. This just ruined my day!" After the guys went into their room he went down the hall and knocked on their door. As they opened it he greeted them with, "I'm the #####in' old bald-headed priest who lives down the hall from you. My name is Fr. B. What's yours?" They immediately knew this was a different kind of priest and so began a different kind of relationship.

"The saints surprise us, they confound us, because by their lives they urge us to abandon a dull and dreary mediocrity." (#138) [2] Fr. B's version of sainthood is anything but mediocre!

What is it about him that makes even the toughest, most cynical student respond? Some have called him the "Dalai Lama of XU" or the priest with the "Buddha-like-face." The childlike part of him is out in front; the adult part of him is more private. Childlike genuineness comes through every time he greets you with, "Well, Hello Saints! What a joy!" His ability to enter this present moment, as if you are the very purpose of his whole day, is disarming whether on campus or at the Norwood Kroger with strangers. You know somehow he truly wants to be there with you. In that moment there is nothing and no one more important than you!

Fr. B with basketball player J.P. Macura, shooting guard who played Division I Basketball for Xavier University over four seasons, 2014–18.
Courtesy of J. P. Macura

Here are Al and XU basketball player J. P. Macura: "Father B has meant the world to me over my years while I was at Xavier. He is the most caring person that I have ever met. Every single time I see him he takes the time to ask me how I am doing, and he truly cares about everyone. Not only do I, but everyone really appreciates what he has done for the university."

Before his ninetieth birthday, Fr. B received a letter from a student he had known twenty years earlier at Brebeuf High School in Indianapolis. "I was so surprised when I met you and got to know you on campus, because you have the kindest face I have ever seen. Seeing your face made something light up in me. My father died when I was five years old and I had been angry ever since. When you said that we are all a gift, and when you called me 'Saint,' it touched me deeply and my anger began to gradually go away."

So maybe we can begin to understand his remarkable charism of *presence*. There is this quality in him that seems to satisfy a basic hunger. The simplest way to describe it is that he connects with the child within each of us. People's faces open wide like a child when they see him. Even if moments later the feeling has passed, the memory of their childlike heart rising up still remains.

People look forward to this startling liberating effect each time they see Fr. B. Others would see this and want it for themselves. An encounter with Fr. B became a ten-second party when you knew you were loved. It's what you hope for with your best friends or your most cherished family members. It doesn't always happen with them. Sometimes we are disappointed.

This man feels genuinely happy to see you. This presence he offers has a sense of "right now" immediacy and urgency. He says all of this in a moment with a delighted look of happiness that you are here and he is here with you. It feels safe, very safe, and protected. The moment is true. The encounter is true. And the moment becomes sacred. And it's hypnotic. You can be yourself without pretense or any mask. Wow! This feels different. It's kind of like what some people have come to call the "Pope Francis effect." We are blessed to have both of these men in our lives.

Fr. B truly lives the art of mindfulness: engaging all of his five senses in the joy of the moment. He has learned that if you are engaged in the present, you can't worry about the past or the future. Creating mindful encounters is his first priority. Nothing bad can happen when he draws you into the present with him. It's a peaceful oasis. In that immediacy something new bursts open and explodes. This is why Fr. B is so blessed to us, because at that moment he is immersed in the Holy Spirit. He's in the dance! "Life is good, and so is Graeter's!" (Graeter's is a Cincinnati ice cream chain. It's his favorite!)

Dr. Ellen Frankenberg, a colleague of his, remembers this story about him as a pastor. As at any parish in the 1970s, Fr. B knew that many of the people of St. Margaret Mary parish struggled to accept their own goodness. In his compassion for them, every night after dinner he would go to the back porch of the rectory and ask God to give general absolution to all of North College Hill! Actually, he was not at all sure of what he was supposed to be doing as a pastor there but God told him, "Just walk around and build trust." And that's just what he did.

In her role as Director of Faith Formation for Bellarmine parish, Jane Myers had the opportunity each year to invite Fr. B to come to our retreat preparing families for the Sacrament of Reconciliation for the first time. She would recruit a willing parent to do a role play with Fr. B demonstrating how to go to confession. To begin, he always wanted to know something personal about the child, "So tell me how things are going at home and at school." The children also loved watching one of the moms or dads pretend to be a ten-year-old, confessing a typical ten-year-old's behaviors like lack of gratitude, not cleaning up the bedroom, fights with a sibling, etc. Fr. B would respond gently and compassionately. They got it. They understood what this sacred moment really means. Preparing with him made all the difference.

Richard Bollman, S.J., former pastor of Bellarmine Chapel, writes about his brother Jesuit this way:

January 1, just two years ago, I decided to go on up to the ten o'clock Mass at Bellarmine. Al Bischoff was presiding, making it a safe bet, nothing but the prayer, the simple truth of it, the start of the year, the praise and trust in the prayers, and attention paid as well to Mary Mother of God, a day for her. About seventy or so people were there, familiar faces, smiles among some from a New Year's Eve party that ended just 8 hours earlier. Al was fully himself and at ease, which is what he brings to leading worship, and regardless of some weariness too, self-doubt and worry in the public eye almost always, this is never allowed to hold him back, or intrude upon his presence with people. I was so relieved to be there, to engage this odd holy day, the call to prayer on the first day of the year.

What is this spirit he transmits? A kind of confidence in love, God's love but also his own. He just allows it to show, glad to count on the spirit of God in everybody, letting it all come to the fore, to show how we can trust. He began, of course, with a welcome to us, "Saints, blessings to you now, happy New Year." People say lately he is slower. Even so, he draws us in to his pacing, where all is well, exceedingly well.

His face is more craggy, I'm thinking. I sat there aware of his being 90-and-a-few years old, ten-and-a-few years older than me. He makes me feel invited to live long and to love well each day, always the result of any conversation with him. And at the homily, having confessed that he'd be repeating some thoughts from Mass the evening before, he opened a passage from Paul to the Colossians that means a lot to him. Chapter 3, that tender blessing of the early community, "you are God's chosen ones" ("think of it he says," tasting it within, letting it matter to everybody, "the chosen ones of God"). And then, "You are his saints, he loves you ... be clothed today with compassion and patience, kindness for everyone, whether you get along with them easily or not." So he spins it out, as it comes from his prayer. He seems to me to be praying all the time, that inward look, and the sheer gratitude with which he lives these days, these late days of his long-struggling life. And he tells of an undergraduate fellow a few years ago who sat down with him, and said, "Fr. B. I just want to thank you for being so kind to us."

Kindness is his gift, in taking time, opening time. In my own visits to him, he has been partly a confessor. I have found his impatience rises only when I might be self-blaming or fretful for who I am. He would shush that devil out of the room. No time for it. For us who live in community with him these years, since 1998, he is so gracious always, in his way of being a channel of grace. He relaxes a room of Jesuits when he arrives, not saying much, but being simply present, and alert and knowing who we are, that's true, knowing what stirs among us. He puts a group of men at ease. All of us, we who know him, we are put at ease, drawn into life by what he does.

There are over twenty different religions among the almost 5000 Xavier students, many of them drawn to Fr. B's presence on campus. In 2014 an interfaith chapel was set up in Husman Hall. A group of Muslim students who lived in the dorm welcomed the space to gather for their daily prayer. Among the additions to the chapel were a fountain and a place to wash one's feet, even enhancing the sacred space by marking a point on the ceiling toward the direction of Mecca out of respect for the students gathering to pray their *Jumma* each Friday afternoon.

Katie Minning, on the Dorothy Day Center for Faith and Justice staff, remembers that soon Fr. B began to join them. After just several weeks of praying *Jumma* with the students, on one Sunday Fr. B noticed one of the Muslim students at the chapel in time for the 4:00 Mass. When Fr. B afterwards expressed his surprise at seeing him, the student responded, "You have prayed with me, so now I have come to pray with you." Attentive presence. Loving accompaniment. Relationship.

CHAPTER 5

Is There a Heaven, and Will I Be There?

Making An Ash of Themselves

At lunch on Ash Wednesday a couple of students noticed Fr. B sitting in the student dining hall. They asked him to come to their table and then offered this challenge. "Tell John he has to go get ashes today. Tell him he's going to hell if he doesn't get ashes." Fr. B looked at John and asked him if he wanted to get ashes. "No," was his response. "Well, if John doesn't want to get ashes, then he shouldn't get ashes," concluded Fr. B.

The next day John made it a point to find Fr. B, asking him, "Do you think I could really go to hell because I didn't receive ashes?" Fr. B, confidently and lovingly, said, "John, I can assure you that you will be in heaven with Jesus one day. In fact, I'm pretty sure I will get there before you, and when I see you coming I will open the gates to welcome you. And just before you come in I will be sure to pour a whole bucket of ashes on your head!" John laughed with relief and, truly touched, said, "Thanks, Fr. B. I think I'll see you in church on Sunday."

There it is! This story captures the impact Fr. B has had on students and on each of us who knows him.

Are we saints *or* are we sinners? Doesn't it have to be one or the other? Maybe if I never sinned again, then he would be right that I am a Saint. But I continue to struggle. How can I be "normal" and still be a Saint? Once again, Fr. B's proclamation, "Hello Saints!" cuts through all of that, the way Christ did with the people he met.

We don't have to make the "binary" decision about whether we are Saints *or* sinners. We are both sinners who have become Saints and Saints who still sin. If we do not cling to the hope that we are Saints our sins will drag us down. When we fail at living as disciples of Jesus, we can call to mind the calming words from Ash Wednesday, "Return to God and believe the Good News" or "Change your heart and be faithful to the Gospel!"

Fr. B visiting with students and parishioners after Mass at Bellarmine Chapel, 1973–74. *Courtesy of the University Archives and Special Collections, Xavier University Library, Cincinnati, Ohio*

Barbara Rueve Otting continues:

As anyone who knows Fr. B will tell you, the first thing you notice about him is that he calls you "Saint." Initially, it mystifies people, but at the same time they love it. I loved it! When growing up Catholic in the 1950s, sin was much discussed in daily Religion classes. I learned very well that I was flawed and sinful, and I let that rule my view of who I was. Imagine, then, at age sixteen to meet a person who called me "Saint!" Although my first response was, "I'm no saint!" at the same time it felt so good to get the slightest inkling that maybe there was some good to be found in me!

Saints are not born Saints but become Saints by being reborn. Jesus came to call sinners and transforms every sinner into a Saint. In the Gospels, everyone who has been touched by Jesus is a Saint whom he saves. Paul does not hesitate to call us Saints, members of the household of God, because for Paul all hearers of the Word are Saints. Ultimately, Saint-making is a claim and action by God, not by us. Any good that we do overflows from the love of God welcomed and alive in us.

We don't need to worry about being saved. That has already happened. Not because of our efforts or because we're perfect. Fr. B would tell us, "Being holy has nothing to do with being free from sin or being perfect." Jesus Christ is powerful. With every breath we take, Jesus is forgiving us and perfecting us. His life and mission are constantly saving us. The Risen Christ is in us, around us; Christ breathes in each of us as a constant grace.

But don't I have to earn heaven? Every day, though maybe not in these words, we tend to ask ourselves, "Am I enough? Am I good enough? Have I done enough?" The resounding answer from Fr. B is "Saint, you are enough! God loves you just the way you are." Therefore, anything we do to improve ourselves is a gift back to God and to those we love. It's not a requirement. Every positive change, every New Year's resolution, every sincere intention, every new discipline or loving action; every act of mercy and justice; they are all *enough* because God loves us already; already and forever!

Sr. Rose Ann Fleming, Special Assistant to the President with duties in the Athletic Department, gives us a glimpse of Fr. B's relationship with athletes:

> Fr. B has not attended a XU basketball game since 1985. It must have been because of his tender heart. The tension made him too anxious. He really wanted the Muskies to win every game but knew he couldn't do anything to impact the outcome. He would wait until near the time when the game would be ending, then turned on his radio to hear the final score. It was then that he could think about and decide how the athletes and students would most need his support.

> One can look at all aspects of human development to understand what Fr. B accomplished with students. His compassion with people was extraordinary. Especially for non-Catholic students at Augustana and at Xavier, the concept of forgiveness was huge! The way in which they were raised in the faith did not strongly hold up the foundational claim of forgiveness of sin and reconciliation with a merciful God. Fr. B convinced them of God's unconditional love because of his love for them.

In recent history the church has rushed to close the time gap between the death of holy women and men and the declaration that they are "blessed" or "saint." Historically it took centuries for the process of sainthood. It took Elizabeth Ann Seton 150 years following her death to be canonized. Archbishop Oscar Romero died in 1980 and was canonized in March 2017. Pope John Paul II died in April 2005, and was canonized in April of 2014, just nine years later! Other examples are St. Mother Teresa of Calcutta, St. Peter Faber, S.J.; St. Maria Elizabeth Hesselblad, St. Jacques Berthieu, and St. Mariam Baourdy. Yes, indeed, there have been and are Saints among us. You are already a Saint because you are already good. That is your "original blessing!" (See book with this title by Matthew Fox, 2000.) Fr. B says, "I see God all around me in the Saints on the XU campus," then jokingly adds "even if their parents can't quite see them the way I do."

Paradoxically, we are *already* Saints while at the same time called *to become* Saints, as we continue to conform our lives more completely to Christ. The Vatican approves particularly extraordinary Saints whom we honor after a thorough validation process. It is also true that God and the community of the faithful recognize and validate us as Saints just for who we are. Jesus came to call sinners, so we all belong to the Reign of God.

Returning to John's questions about Lent, heaven, and hell, in his homily on the following Sunday, the First Sunday of Lent, Fr. B reflected on the beautiful Gospel of the Samaritan woman at the well. He told the story of the Xavier student John as a clear example of "a conversation at the well," the kind of conversation each of us might have on any day at our workplace, in our home, at the grocery store. It is a story of intimacy and transformation. Just as Jesus listened to the Samaritan woman, told her all about her life without any judgment, and offered her a whole new kind of water, Fr. B has offered the same to us and shown us how to offer simple life and hope to people in our lives. "Many people believed because of the woman's testimony. 'He told me everything I've ever done.'" (Jn. 4: 39)

Here are the remarkable words in the Rite of Baptism, "The Christian community welcomes you with great joy. In its name I *claim you* for Christ our Savior by the sign of the cross. I now trace the sign of the cross on your forehead and I invite your parents and godparents to do the same." [3] These words are spoken as an introduction to the prayer of exorcism at the beginning of the baptismal rite during which the power of Christ is called upon to dispel the power of darkness. Fr. B invites us all to live each moment trusting these life-changing words!

Fr. B baptizing Kathleen Rose Bonilla, daughter of Alejandro and Molly, May 2019. *Courtesy of Jane Myers*

When we hear ourselves called Saints we feel God's grace pouring over us. We intuitively understand its inherent dignity and calling power. We know we are forgiven at every moment because we have already been claimed for Christ!

You could say that at times when Fr. B says, "Hello Saints," there is the sense that a simple exorcism is taking place. From the mouth of this venerable priest of seventy years the demons and the darkness fall back. Satan's prosecution of us in our guilt and shame cannot penetrate the circle of light he has created with and around us. It's as if we are standing with Jesus in the garden when the soldiers come and say they are looking for Jesus of Nazareth. He says, "I am" and they fall back in fear and defeat. As the Christ in Al speaks to the Christ in each of us we are protected and held in this public demonstration of faith, hope, and love.

In the Orthodox Church there is the belief that from Ash Wednesday until the night before Pentecost Sunday there is only a "thin veil" that separates this world from the supernatural. So, there is the understanding that spirits of darkness can move between worlds, while at the same time the Spirit of the risen Christ can be remarkably felt in both. It is for just this straddling of two worlds that Fr. B's belief in us and his proclamation prepare us.

By calling us Saints, Fr. B is imitating the way Paul greeted all Christians in his writings. Paul proclaimed that the early Christians did not become Saints by doing good deeds. He claimed that they were already Saints by the saving act of Jesus so that they could get on with the work of bringing the reign of God to life. Too many Christians have wasted time asking, "Will I go to heaven, or what do I have to do to get there?" Fr. B's proclamation moves us past all of that. Each of us is already a Saint by the most powerful and intimate action of God, so let's get on with living!

Several times every day when Fr. B is in the Gallagher Student Center or the dining hall or the dorm and someone holds the door for him, he looks them right in the eye and says, "Thanks, Saint. I will be there holding the door for you when you get to heaven!"

When he is prayerfully preaching to the community he loves, he adds, "If one of you is not going to be in heaven, then I don't want to be there!" He wonders, how could God be happy if one of God's beloved children is not there?

CHAPTER 6

The True Self: Lori's Story

Lori Bolas shares a memory from her time with Fr. B at Augustana:

I can still hear him saying, 'Hello Saint.' From the moment
I met him, his warmth and sincerity became a lifeline. It
was as though he instantly knew me—the real me—seeing
right through my bubbly outgoing 'college persona'
to the frightened, sad little girl whose life had been
shattered just a year before heading off to Augie.

Having grown up in the theater I was a good actress. Most of my
friends knew nothing of the trauma I'd been through. With Fr. B
any pretense melted away, and I felt instantly accepted, loved, and
safe. Around Fr. B it was as though God was speaking through him
directly to me, telling me it would be OK—despite the tragedies
I had kept hidden from the world. Not only did Fr. B's friendship
help to heal emotional wounds, it taught me life lessons that I still
carry today. He showed me daily the absolute power of a simple
smile and a friendly gesture. Fr. B seemed to elevate everyone
around him—no matter their walk in life. He taught me that one

warm word (even if it is the same one over and over again, 'Saint!'), one smile can save the day. And most importantly, he showed us all that people matter, no matter how different we are. At the end of the day we are all 'Saints' to Fr. B, and of course to God.

Fr B brought me closer to God than I had ever been. My faith journey is now rich, and I know beyond a shadow of a doubt that God brought me to Augie to meet Fr. B. Though baptized Catholic, my family never went to church. After meeting him I never missed a single Mass. I went to Bible study and was even confirmed at Augustana. To sum it up, thanks to Fr. B, I truly believe I had the opportunity to see God in action. Father B emanated love. God is love. Fr. B is also the Saint that he believes is in all of us!

Here's the way Fr. Richard Rohr describes Lori's experience:

Searching for and rediscovering the True Self is the fundamentum, the essential task that will gradually open us to receiving and giving love to God, others, and ourselves ... You (and every other created thing) begin with your unique divine DNA, an inner destiny as it were, an absolute core that knows the truth about you ... an *Imago Dei* that begs to be allowed, to be fulfilled, and to show itself. [4]

This is your *True Self.* Historically, it was often called *'the soul.'"* [5]

St. Paul says it another way. You were chosen in Christ before the world was made—to stand before God in love—marked out beforehand as fully adopted sons and daughters. (Eph. 1: 4-5) Those fully adopted sons and daughters, those persons created in the image of

God, those True Selves—these are names for the Saints who we already are. Fr. B has known that instinctively. This attitude and belief with which he named us drove his daily practice and behavior and his constant prayer for us.

Fifty years ago Thomas Merton first introduced the term "True Self" that has since become a touchstone for spiritual seekers east and west:

> A Zen master would call the True Self 'the face we had before
> we were born.' Paul would call it who you are 'in Christ, hidden
> in God' (Colossians 3:3). It is who you are before having done
> anything right or anything wrong, who you are before having
> thought about who you are. Thinking creates the false self,
> the ego self, the insecure self. The God-given contemplative
> mind, on the other hand, recognizes the God Self, the Christ
> Self, the True Self of abundance and deep inner security.
> We start with mere seeing; we end up with recognizing. [6]

This "True Self" is known by God and knows God even before we are born. The paradox of growing up includes the challenge to stay in touch with and to make conscious the True Self even as our ego constructs a survivable life with our worldly skills. Fr. B's gift of presence, as Richard Rohr suggests, moves us to walk and breathe each day from our Truer Self.

Many of us reading this have demonstrated excellent worldly skills. We have not only survived. We have thrived and built a life that many would admire. Others may not have been that successful. But under any scenario there are many moments in life when we so badly need our True Self. This is when the invitation of "Hello Saint" rises again.

From Katie Minning, at Xavier's Center for Faith and Justice and longtime friend of Fr. B:

After you spend time with Fr. B you have the sense that he is no longer 'that priest.' He is just your friend. I remember when Fr. B, along with Brother Burns, began quiet retreats for seniors. Each spring before they graduated, groups of twelve seniors would go away together for several days. He would teach them how to quietly sit in God's presence. One student, an art major, created her senior thesis out of her deep experience of prayer during her retreat. It was her final step as she left Xavier, integrating into her art what she had learned about herself and about God's intimate love for her.

Fr. B in the homecoming parade.
Courtesy of Xavier University

Whether at Elder High School, serving a parish, or at Augustana, Brebeuf, or Xavier, Fr. B has had a way of connecting us with one another and with God who loves us. Because he possesses a scrupulous humility and guileless gratitude, he has been an open channel of love and blessing. His True Self got stronger over the years in surrender to his loving God because he kept believing in it. He invites us to do the same. Patience, perseverance, and prayer will empower the authority and leadership of our True Self within us.

Longtime friend and Jesuit companion Darrell Burns writes:

> He does not tell you what to do. He simply recognizes the goodness in you and encourages you to keep growing, but without any expectations. He says, 'I want to walk with you.' It's not that I imitate him. Instead, I find his life to be an inspiration. He instills in me a desire to live the way he lives, nonjudgmentally and with a broader view of life. He inspires me to live my life by using and sharing my unique gifts and reaching for happiness. He is a touchstone for me when we talk or share a meal, then he goes on and I am more free to do what I need to do.

Because of his active always-all-day prayer life, he is able to understand the Gospel vividly in his delightful encounters with others and able to more clearly articulate the joy of the Gospel in his preaching. One of his top five favorite Scriptures is "I have come that they may have life, and have it more abundantly." (Jn.10:10) He committed himself to living this Good News every day. When he would have memories of trauma or become depressed or confused he knew his thoughts had entered a dangerous neighborhood he should stay away from. With a resonant dismissal of those demons he would step out into the sunshine to find one of us so he could celebrate the truth and the light.

Ultimately, the True Self (the "Saint" in us) cannot be hurt. It has nothing to prove, nothing to protect. It is indestructible because it is our very being in God, the great I am (Ex. 3:4), living in and through each of us. This is the passionate proclamation and resolute hope that Fr. B gives us as his legacy gift. Remember, this book is *for* us, *from* him. Picture the twinkle in his eye smiling at us as he meets us on the path.

Does any of this make us uncomfortable? Does it scandalize us to think that sin does not matter as much? Sin is from the false self, and the false self cannot live forever. Only the True Self, only love, will survive. In the end, only the True Self is real. Everything else dies with us when our mortal bodies die.

When we talked with Fr. B about this chapter, he said it succinctly, "You have to come home to yourself in order to find your real self. Then you find the Holy One, the one God made you to be."

CHAPTER 7
Self Is Sacred

We highly recommend reading *Self Therapy: A Step-By-Step Guide to Creating Wholeness and Healing Your Inner Child Using IFS (Internal Family Systems)*, by Jay Earley, Ph.D. (and others books about IFS). In its foreword, the founder of IFS Therapy, Richard Schwartz, says the following:

> As you relate to even your most shameful emotions and impulses with curiosity rather than judgment and with caring rather than disgust, you will find that these parts of you are not what they seem. They are valuable inner resources that have been distorted by difficult life experiences. Even more uplifting, you will learn that you have a core, an essence that is untouched by life's traumas. What IFS calls the Self is in every one of us; it is a source of wonderful qualities from which we can lead our inner and outer lives ... not just coping with but actually transforming emotions and beliefs. One may not be able to unburden all one's exiles, but one can reverse the atmosphere of the inner world from one of self-loathing to self-love and self-leadership.[7]

An encounter with Fr. B in a way becomes an encounter with Self which is where Christ resides within each of us. B has a uniquely disarming and easily underestimated way of bringing us into a huddle with Self who is nonjudgmental, compassionate, and curious. Neither Christ nor Fr. B *pathologizes* people. We have the resources within ourselves for healing and conversion in Christ. The trajectory of the Holy Spirit is clear: love, wisdom, and connectedness.

Fr. B is in every way a Catholic Jesuit priest. He has a way of connecting us with a spirituality that is bigger and more universal than any category. We all have many parts. Some are hurt; some used to help us but now hold us back. But at our core and rising up throughout life is a Self that is untouched. The risen Christ resides there, in our DNA, and makes all the difference. If we are open and welcoming, we can meet the risen Christ within us. Then we will be on the path toward evangelizing and healing our parts.

At our core the Universal Christ is calling forth our own Self, our soul. When the two meet more consciously in us we awaken and begin an exciting and transformative journey. Again, patience, perseverance, and prayer will make this a holy pilgrimage toward our true home. Christ and I walk together. This is the path of discipleship.

If we approach all of our parts with the love of Christ together with Self, the wounded will receive the compassion and healing Christ has to offer. Fr. B was forced to learn this. He had no choice. He had to learn this or die. He still has exiles and protectors inside who cause him grief, but underneath it all is his True Self in the Risen Christ. From this place of strength and grace, he introduces people to their own True Self, often with a growing awareness of what he is calling forth and celebrating in us.

Years ago a group of students came to Fr. B to ask if he would offer a quiet, reflective Mass at 4:00 PM in the afternoon as an alternative to the 10:00 PM student Mass. For years, Sunday after Sunday, he has presided at this Mass. It became the practice that on the Sunday of a holiday weekend there would not be a 4:00 PM Mass since students would still be travelling back to campus. On one of those Sunday afternoons Fr. B walked up to the chapel to pray quietly alone. Soon, five or six students showed up, expecting Mass. "Well, Saints, since you are all here, let's have Mass!"

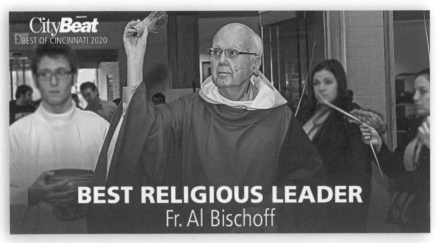

City Beat magazine, Cincinnati, Ohio, Cover 2020.
Courtesy of the University Archives and Special Collections, Xavier University Library, Cincinnati, Ohio

Each Sunday at the 4:00 PM Mass, when Fr. B says, "Now listen, Saints ..." the students know he is talking to each one of them. You can hear an "active quiet" in the chapel, the sound of each person actively listening with full attention. What he says is not always new, but it is as if it's the first time they are hearing it. He talks to them right where they are, welcoming them and instilling in each of them an affirming sense of importance. He knows and understands what is going on in the students' lives. When he preaches, he offers some context for the Scriptures, then focuses on what the Gospel says to us about who we are.

Every single part of us is connected to the Self, even if it seems isolated or in a protected cocoon. Every part has an umbilical cord to Christ and Self. Christ is rising from the dead in us, causing an insurrection of joy and hope and love, and, of course, faith. We get excited about this uprising and we feel it in people like Fr. B. The Christ in him calls out to the Christ in us. The True Self does the same. Each time, an unbreakable loop is being installed within us.

This book was not written to create a fan club for Fr. B. It was written to help us remember how we felt in his presence and to learn how to re-create that experience in our contact with each person we meet every day. Our Christ-Self rises up through all the darkness in us and reaches out to touch another. This is an invitation to their Christ-Self to rise up and meet ours. It is a moment of recognition and celebration. It is an awakened feeling of home, a glimpse of the reign of God.

Think of John the Baptist leaping in the womb of Elizabeth when Mary came to visit her. The Christ-Self in John within Elizabeth recognized the Christ-Self within Mary's womb. Later John would recognize Christ in the same way at his baptism in the Jordan. The skies would open and a voice would be heard, "This is my beloved Son." This happens to us when we embrace the Christ-Self. Our True Self says to us with confidence, "You are beloved." We know this to be true! If we begin each day with humility and gratitude, centering ourselves in Sacred Self, we will be awake and alert to living as true disciples.

CHAPTER 8

Our Coping Self, Our "as if" Self

(often referred to as the *false self*)

We are all sinners. We are all Saints. The True Self grows stronger in us each day under God's love and protection. We pray for this for our children, for each other especially those we love, and especially at the moment of death. God and Self will never leave us. "Come, Lord Jesus, embrace the best of me to live forever with you. Let the rest fall away, the useless shell and remains of my coping self."

There is no direct path to the True Self except on the back of the false self. It's like Jesus riding on a donkey into Jerusalem. Our innocence as a child becomes compromised by the normal, healthy developmental drive of the ego to build a container, our coping self, the person we unfortunately believe is me.

Every A+ we get, every trophy we win, every pat on the back, every achievement may be good, but it may also be a distraction from Self. Our two-dimensional repertoire becomes tiresome and annoying to ourselves and others. But at some point we have collected enough trophies. We have achieved a career and maybe a family, and at the height of the ego's glory a growing doubt presents itself. We begin to see our coping self with more objectivity and with some detachment.

Are all of the ego's achievements really so important? Or were they just the donkey that our True Self rode on to mid-life and to the most important tasks of our lives? We have lost the innocence of childhood, and the ego has taken us as far as it can rightfully go. We must detach from the false self, as valuable as it has been. If we let it continue to assert itself as our dominant persona, it may make us into a caricature of ourselves. Our shell can become increasingly obvious to others, too. Our substance can become hidden, and that's sad.

A gnawing hunger for the Sacred Self begins as a critical experience. Letting ourselves stay with the hunger eventually becomes a holy habit.

This is what Jesus meant by "You must be born again." We all have seen people strut and fret their way past mid-life on the strength of their ego alone. We cannot regain our innocence. We must meet God in ourselves and together we can coax the True Self to express itself in our prayer, in our relationships, and in our service. But this "Saint" in us has to struggle for dominance with the usurping energy of the ego. As the Twelve Steps have taught us, only our Higher Power can restore us to sanity.

Years ago, members of a particular fraternity were in trouble. They came to Fr. B to tell him that because of their behavior they were on the verge of suspension. Their fear inspired a creative "plea bargain." They asked Fr. B if they could propose to the administration that he would lead them on a private directed weekend retreat in lieu of suspension. Wow! Their remorse was calling them to take time in prayer, led by someone they knew would guide them to a forgiving God. The administration agreed, and so began the annual "senior silent retreats." Those experiences at the Jesuit Renewal Center in Milford created a beautiful and intriguing bond between the students and Fr. B.

It is in this mid-life struggle that Fr. B's proclamation that we are Saints becomes a fulfilled prophecy if we allow it. Mostly, it involves receiving God's grace rather than doing anything ourselves. Being willing to wait and be patient and to receive this revealed True Self goes against the grain of the ego and the false self, but the satisfactions of the process are deeply rewarding. It is particularly at this transition point that a spiritually skilled therapist or spiritual director can be an ally to the assertion of the True Self. Once the True Self is in charge, the blessings and freedoms of graceful aging bring new life and hope, new humility and gratitude. It is a quiet revolution that we each will experience as we embrace the Risen Christ in ourselves and in each other.

Those whose lives and egos have been crushed are often closer to the reign of God than those who have been privileged and entitled. The crushed are capable of true humility and dependence on God. Some survivors of childhood trauma have been able to develop an intimacy with a God who made them feel safe. Such individuals may have maintained a moral compass and often developed a transparency to the True Self even from an early age. And if their ego has not necessarily been gratified that much by the world, if their ego has been ready to accept the risky and mature executive functioning of their True Self at mid-life, then they can become the truly charismatic change agents and remarkable people we all have known and celebrated.

Such a person by general acclamation is Fr. Al Bischoff. But he has suffered every single day. The lifelong pain of a traumatized childhood and a sometimes thwarted ego have resulted in benefits to others, exceptional and far-reaching. In recent years he has experienced increased personal freedom and peace. But there are still moments at 3:00 AM when he is haunted by the ghosts of frightening trauma and an un-reassured ego. That is when he prays from his crushed self with radical dependence on God, naturally leading him to pray for all of us. Many saints and holy persons throughout history have likewise suffered for their gifts of bringing Christ into their daily world.

(Continuing Frank Evans' reflection.) We all have seen a glimpse of what B has been through. He describes himself as a broken and healed man. I think that's true. And that's where he gets his strength and his ability to reach deep into all of us. I know he is at peace now and tries to share that gift of peace with all of us.

Through it all, we weren't naive ... we knew B was not your ordinary priest going through the motions. There was something innately spiritual about him. When he spoke of his weaknesses they were ones each of us struggled with as well. It made you realize how frail we all are and how we need to have a closer relationship with God. Is there anybody who after talking with B didn't feel better? Didn't feel a burden lifted? I think this is the gift B gives us all. His calm and unassuming manner rubs off on all of us.

B just celebrated his 93rd birthday. I am positive that one day he will hear God say "Welcome home my good and faithful disciple."

Listen to Thomas Merton's words from *New Seeds of Contemplation:*

Every one of us is shadowed by an illusory person: a false self. This is the person that I want myself to be but who cannot exist, because God—because Truth, Light—knows nothing about the false self. And to be unknown to God is altogether too much privacy. My false and private self is the one who wants to exist outside the reach of God's will and God's love—outside of reality and outside of life. And such a self cannot help but be an illusion. To be a saint means to be my true self. Therefore the problem of sanctity and salvation is in fact the problem of finding out who I truly am and of discovering my true self, my essence or core. [8]

Richard Rohr writes:

[Merton] did this to clarify for many Christians the meaning of Jesus' central and oft-repeated teaching that we must die to ourselves, or "lose ourselves to find ourselves" (Mark 8:35). Jesus' admonition has caused much havoc and pushback in Christian history because it sounds negative and ascetical, and it was usually interpreted as an appeal to deny the body. But the full intent is personal liberation, not self-punishment. Merton rightly recognized that it was not the body that had to "die" but the "false self" which is always an imposter posing for "me." [9]

The fundamental and complex task of finding our True Self means engaging and confronting those parts of ourselves which hold us back and even sabotage us. That which is best in all of us and certainly that which is such a bright light in Fr. B believes in our True Self, whom he called "Saint."

To close these thoughts, here's a paradox. Although it's helpful to distinguish between the false or coping self and the True Self, our prayers will lead us to a place where we will accept and

Al at Bellarmine Chapel all-parish Mass September 9, 2012.
Courtesy of Rich Sofranko

love them both. Self now becomes confident and we experience trust and peace. We no longer need the duality of false self and True Self. We are each one person in Christ with our compromised history but embracing our joyful destiny. We no longer fear. We are increasingly more free to receive and to give love. Finally, with our last breath, we can say with Jesus, "It is finished" and fall into the arms of our Creator, now finally home.

Some reflections to take to prayer:

- Do I recognize the image and likeness of God in my own DNA, in every cell of my body? Is the image of God in my True Self, my soul?

- If my True Self already knows the Risen Christ, then what is my false self striving and straining for?

- St. Francis of Assisi felt sorry for the pitiful coping self. He named it "Brother Ass" who wanted to keep the best food for himself, who did not want to get up and serve others, who just wanted to be left alone. Do you feel sorry for your false self? (This is a good question because it is the beginning of compassion for ourselves and for all the rest of groaning suffering humanity.)

- The Dalai Lama says, "Pain is inevitable but suffering is optional." Can we distinguish these? Here's the difference—in one way we are the vulnerable witness to our genuine wounds, which gives us graced wisdom. The rest is sound and fury, which we may indulge at the risk of permanent self-pity and resentment. What is the real pain in my life and what is simply the drama and suffering of "Brother Ass" or "Sister Ass," our coping self?

- If my True Self is my "soul" that will live forever, can I begin to let go of my false self, which often reveals itself in self-pity, resentment, anger, fear, and shame? How can I let go of judgment of others, judgment of myself?

- How can I let go of my attachments and addictions which make me feel ashamed or resentful or both, which only distract me from my True Self?

- What at this very moment would help me to identify more and more with the True Self and let go of the false self?

- Who can help me in this quest?

Some practices that Fr. B would encourage include:

- More frequent reception of the Eucharist in Communion and sitting in prayer before the Blessed Sacrament, responding to the intimate invitation that is always offered.

- Accessing the daily Scripture readings of the church and practicing *Lectio Divina*. (See Appendix of resources.)

- Opening up to discernment and consolation through the Sacrament of Reconciliation.

- Learning and practicing mindfulness, meditation, centering prayer, contemplative prayer.

- Praying *The Spiritual Exercises of St. Ignatius.*

- Deepening our understanding of ourselves with a trusted and qualified lay spiritual companion, pastoral psychotherapist, or spiritual director.

CHAPTER 9

Surviving Childhood
as a Child of the Light

Many of us as children had experiences of being surrounded by darkness, then instinctively reaching for and moving toward the light. Even in their confusion and fear of the dark, some children figure this out at a very young age.

Dark things do happen to children. Those who are not broken by them often have developed a relationship with God as the only power and presence who could provide safety when they are frightened. Even very young children can call out from their hearts to God for comfort. They may not understand how it works, but they know that God is much bigger than, and is a true alternative to, any darkness. Even if they are not spared atrocities and pain, they instinctively embrace the truth that God's consoling presence and love are holding them.

Christina Noble was such a child. As a little girl growing up in the slums of Ireland, one of eight children, six of whom survived, she learned how to hold body and soul together. Her mother died when she was ten, but even before that, she, like Fr. B, had discovered the consolation of singing. She fell in love with Doris Day songs and other popular songs on the radio. When things were bleakest she would argue with God, but still sing. She was not spared abuse and humiliation, but she was strengthened into the woman she became. Today her foundation cares for more than 700,000 orphans in Vietnam.

As we have alluded to previously, Fr. B suffered indescribable chronic abuse as a child, living every day since with the consequences of trauma. There are parts of him that still carry the pain and terror. This is important, not for shock value, but because it is his brave journey that has made him a singular presence in our lives. He found freedom and peace and a loving God. He prays for the same for each of us.

It turns out that Fr. B's experience of brokenness was a lot like that of a man who lived 400 years earlier, Ignatius of Loyola. As a Jesuit, Fr. B knew that his struggles resembled St. Ignatius' own battle in the cave at Manresa. Margaret Silf describes it:

> He makes a 'home' for himself in a cave near the river. Alone, in this bleak place, he begins to meet his own 'demons.' Here the insights of his dream-time in Loyola are put to the test in the cold light of day. He is to discover for himself the true force of the 'destructive spirits' of spiritual desolation as well as the overwhelming joy that only the 'creative spirits' of spiritual consolation can bring. In the Manresa months, Ignatius is, as it were, living in his own personal wilderness, which exposes him to the extremes of his own personality, as well as to the depths of God's love. There in the cave he experiences the very best of himself and the very worst ... He begins to notice the dynamic of God's love operating in his heart, and to realize that when his focus is on himself, and his past and present failures and sinfulness, real or imagined, the destructive movements are likely to overwhelm him and paralyze all his efforts for good. When his focus is on God, however, and on the world around him with all its needs and longings, he notices

that the creative movements within him will restore him to the sense of vocation that has led him this far on his journey. [10]

Ignatius emerged from the cave of his struggle having written what we know as "The Spiritual Exercises," a powerful self-examination and prayer process which has fortified Fr. B over all his years in the Company of Jesus. He, too, as a man of prayer and as a Jesuit, struggled with destructive spirits of desolation and worked daily to focus on a creative spirituality of consolation. This is not an easy process for anyone.

It does not happen with every trauma victim, but for Fr. B the grace of God has been extremely consoling and has created a capacity in him for ecstatic joy. That word "ecstatic" literally means "to stand outside oneself." Behavioral health experts sometimes use the word "dissociation." Fr. B's survival as a child required that he "dissociate" from his body when he experienced violation that he could not understand.

Although post-traumatic stress disorder almost broke him at several critical moments in his life, skilled and loving psychiatrists, counselors, colleagues, and friends and a deep prayer life helped him move toward a real but vulnerable place of light. He has known suffering and the dark side of humanity but he has always embraced the light he found in the Risen Christ and the Good News of the Reign of God. That has been a lasting and perfect match: suffering for joy. This is why he knows so intimately the new creation that Jesus came to proclaim.

Take a moment and write on a page, maybe in your journal,
times when you have felt desolation, abandonment, or
rejection and how you found your way to the Light.

Even though one may be happy and well-adjusted now, our human experience has taught us that to live is to suffer. We may or may not have suffered the kind of trauma Fr. B did, but we probably have been misunderstood or neglected. We may have been deeply hurt or have experienced great losses.

Fr. B got up every day and chose *not* to be a victim. He trusted that God could use his brokenness. What an amazing thing! He believed that the darkness in his own life was exactly where he looked for God and where God allowed the light to come through to console and strengthen him and others. Even if we did not know these details about his life and suffering, his urgent clinging to the light has refreshed us, too. The miracle is that we, like Fr. B, are drawn to the light and carry the light to our families and friends. That is his witness to us. That's why we, like him, are living as Saints. Fr. B wants us to remember that this book is about us and our journey, too. By living this way, at the end of our lives everything within us will want to run toward the Light and know with full confidence that we have arrived home.

CHAPTER 10

Wrestling with Angels, Wrestling with Demons

Stay sober and alert. Your opponent the devil is prowling like a roaring lion looking for someone to devour. (1 Peter 5: 8)

A story about himself which Fr. B told years ago was that he was on a day trip with his good friend, Leo Klein, S.J., to Metamora, Indiana. They were browsing through collections created by local artists. Fr. B's eyes were drawn to a painting of a tree which had been hit by lightning. The tree was seared and scorched. He continued on, taking in many other works of art, but found himself returning to this very particular painting. He decided to buy it. He brought it home and hung it up on his wall. After several days of sitting with the painting he was overcome with the realization that he was the tree. He just broke down and wept. He, too, had been scorched and seared by the startling jolts of trauma, cauterized and scarred by the intensity of fire in his own life.

It was in his adult life he realized he had been violated in a number of ways, in fact, abused by several different perpetrators. The tension among parts inside helped him to identify with the brokenness of the world sooner and more clearly than most people. One of

Framed scorched tree Al bought in Metamora, Indiana.

his parts, *the guilty one,* was always afraid and panicked around male authority figures. Another part, *the loyal one,* was often compulsively obedient to people and institutions in his life. And *the perfect one* was always needing to look good by the way he dressed and acted so he could not be criticized or questioned.

In some ways, Fr. B's gift of presence came from learned eager-
ness to please. He wanted acceptance so badly that others had a special power and believability. The past was not safe. The future was
unknown. He himself needed the safety of the present moment. He
made that safety happen in each encounter with others. He turned
his fears into a charism to draw people in the present moment into
the freedom of the Holy Spirit. And he lived the present abundantly
with each of us.

People hear this truth when they hear him preach. They really
hear the Good News from one who is poor in spirit, not one who is
defined by a big ego. Hounded by guilt, he remains alert and humble; broken, he remains childlike and hope-filled. That is his charism
born from suffering.

Colin Carney, Rugby President, 2017 and 2018, and Jose Sanchez,
team member, write about their experience:

> Fr. B had a great impact on the rugby team, always checking
> in on how the team was doing when he would see me in my
> rugby gear or sweats on campus. Each home game he would
> make his way down to the 'pitch' just before kick and the
> team would gather around him. He would lead us in prayer,
> always making us laugh when he reminded us of the biblical
> David vs. Goliath story and how David "kicked Goliath's ass."
> Since we were always the smaller team my freshman year,
> the image and his prayer strengthened our confidence. He
> certainly left a lasting impression. We miss those interactions.

Clearly, Fr. B chose the familiar and iconic biblical story of David and Goliath to invite the team to imagine themselves as stronger
than any opponent, to convert their anxiety about facing behemoth

opponents into a courage bigger than themselves. We need this same courage to face the darkness in ourselves.

Al at all-parish Mass September 9, 2012.
Courtesy of Rich Sofranko

As a struggling survivor, Fr. B suffered several emotional breakdowns. There is no shame in this. He worked with psychiatrists and psychotherapists over the years in a way that required him to stand beside himself and look at trauma more objectively. This work saved him from remaining fundamentally broken. He was able to do this because he was already a skillful observer of human nature and because of the deep appreciation he had for friends and other significant people in his life. All this allowed him to actively use an observing self in his homilies, often with humor, to connect with the vulnerabilities of all those listening to him—those of all genders, all ages, all economies, all orientations.

Thousands of people have been attracted to Fr. B's Masses, to his preaching, and to him as a confessor and spiritual director. Few people have lived more consistently in the breach between subjective pain and the rational self. Even in his 90s he struggled with the long-term effects of abuse. Destructive thoughts continued to erupt and assault him. "You have no rights." "You are responsible." "You caused this." Like many survivors, he said that he wished he could grieve for his younger self.

During his first retreat with Bill Creed, S.J., in the 1970s, he began the painful yet necessary work of facing his awful experiences. Much later in his years, Fr. B became more and more like Simeon and Anna in the Temple. They were blessed with long life and the eyes to recognize the Savior they had been waiting for. He saw the truth being victorious over the lies which pursued him his whole life.

Fr. B's wounds kept him totally dependent on God. In order to survive, Fr. B had to cling to the Lord and, in a way, to evangelize all the parts of himself. As he modeled, so each of us is invited to identify and describe the parts in us that still need to hear the Good News and the promise of grace and healing. This is the trajectory of freedom that brings us—the Saints—into the Reign of God.

The word *mystic* means "eyes turned inward." There have been throughout history many hermits, monks, holy women and men who have exemplified the interior life. St. Benedict wrote about turning one's heart, mind, and eyes to the deifying light of God which transforms us from the inside. An amazing thing about Fr. B is that his chronic brokenness inside was like the cell of a monk where he lived alone with the suffering Jesus, all the while projecting to us the persona of one who walked in joy.

There have been many paradoxes in Fr. B's inner and his outer worlds. God used him as a broken man. Although he lacked confidence, the ways in which God gave him courage were truly exceptional. We all witnessed this during his presiding and preaching. We might call it the "charism of vulnerability." Henri Nouwen would describe it as the behavior of a "wounded healer." Fr. B made his message embraceable to us because he always acknowledged his own inadequacies. He always thought that other Jesuits were more eloquent academically or in their theological exposition. He always started from that place in him where God could really reach him, and through him reach all of us.

There was a similar spirit in Ghandi, Martin Luther King, Jr., Mother Teresa, Elie Wiesel, Pope Francis, and other survivors who have used their suffering as a sensitive template for proclaiming a just and loving society. If we only stay with our pain, we are just victims. But if we rise up from our pain and join the Risen Christ who still bears his wounds, then the process of living grace and sanctification can do its work over our lifetime. Then we live out of our true identity as divine children of God. Then we can burst forth into compassion for others. Then the Saints can come marching into a dark and needy world.

As a child and young man, Fr. B had been scraped out like a pumpkin, so close to the skin that he could be filled with light, but not so much that he would collapse on himself. He has been resilient. His proclamation to all is of joy, regardless of circumstances, regardless of religious or ethnic background. The joy is authentic and palpable because its source is the tortured self of a lonely child who was transformed into a redeemed and healed adult soaring in the hope of the Risen Christ! Fr. B wants each of us to search for the Risen Christ in ourselves and in all those we meet each day.

CHAPTER 11

Through Brokenness to Maturity

While at Augustana, Fr. B often prayed, "I'm in my fifties, pot-bellied, and balding, but I'm all you've got, Lord, so use me!" Could I possibly compose a similar prayer to God about myself?

During Advent one year, in a homily he reminded us that God came to earth to better understand the human beings God had created. Each of us is broken, yes, but each of us is also perfect. Our Creator could not produce anything less. We live always straddling the two realities of our perfection and our vulnerability. Living in this paradox is one of the challenges of maturity.

Accepting and embracing our own vulnerability is essential to being able to love others in their brokenness as perfectly loveable. Humility, brokenness, and respect are fundamental to our healthy humanity. You may recall that Fr. B expresses this in his self-effacing humor and his choice to forget himself and always delight in the present interaction with each person.

Again, borrowing from *Rejoice and Be Glad*:

Not everything a saint says is completely faithful to the Gospel;
not everything he or she does is authentic or perfect. What we

need to contemplate is the totality of their life, their entire journey of growth in holiness, the reflection of Jesus Christ that emerges when we grasp their overall meaning as a person. (#22)[11]

Our very human condition often keeps us ashamed of our brokenness. We hide it from ourselves and from each other. We even try to hide it from God. Living in denial and in shame cuts us off from community, from intimacy, and from our own spiritual life. Denial and shame can also push us toward addictions and provide fertile ground for the false self to assert its power. Other demons then find their way in: self-pity, resentment, jealousy, anger, scorn, prejudice, isolation, lust, and greed.

The only relief is to explore our vulnerabilities and brokenness and to embrace them as the way in for God and others to love us. We cannot receive love if we're hiding. We cannot give love if we're hiding. We cannot pray if we're hiding. We cannot grow if we're hiding. Shame fuels the false self. Shame can be of our own making or a curse inflicted by neglect or abuse from those who should have been our caregivers.

The curse that almost broke Fr. B was knowing from an early age that he was broken and not being able to hide from it or deny it. He brought his broken reality with humility and obedience to God and offered his life in service to others. With the help of psychiatry, psychotherapy, and spiritual direction he was able to find some stability and acceptance. As he matured he even embraced it and said, "Thank you, God, for things just as they are."

The freedom that grew from that prayer made it possible for him to feel the pain of others and to speak the good news out of his own joy at having been accepted by God in spite of everything. A broken vessel can channel life. Our broken selves and our True Self can co-exist. Gratitude and humility release the freedom in all of us to channel love and service.

Fr. B laughingly talks about himself in the third person, saying, "You know Albert has to look good," or "Albert wouldn't be Albert if he didn't have something to feel guilty about." He knows himself and accepts his personality like an annoying roommate who is always there. So he loves him. In doing all this he gives us a model for our own living and aging that we too can embrace. Accepting our weakness before God is key to loving ourselves and others. Humility and gratitude and trust will eventually drive away all the demons of the false self. Persistence, patience and prayer win out over time.

If we stop hiding in shame and embrace the mystery, we will discover the freedom to forgive our parents, siblings, and children; as well as to forgive our lovers, our friends, and our enemies; and to forgive ourselves. Everyone is broken; everyone is perfect; everyone is to blame; everyone is forgiven. "And just possibly, everyone is going to heaven. That is a good and holy thing to hope for," according to St. John Paul II.

We have noted that as a young man in the 1940s, Fr. B was rejected by the draft board. He returned to Xavier University and later entered the seminary. He said to God, "I know I'm a mess and I know I'm broken, but maybe you could use me somehow." He committed himself to a fearless childlike obedience, and this commitment forced him to become discerning. He discovered that to celebrate the present moment in contact with others was a safer place than his own inner world. He learned that entering the present moment with others was a sacred place for everyone. That became his specialty. Perhaps that's why it's so important that we even care about his legacy.

Is this unique? Is it really true? It may sound a bit grandiose, but could it also be sacred? For those who know Fr. B, we propose it is worth reflecting on this mindful way of living. Entering the present moment can be a liberating oasis of joy for any individual. It truly becomes sacramental when it is shared with others in relationship, in community, or wherever it happens.

Joe Wheeler, who knew Fr. B at Augustana, writes:

> The thing I remember most about Fr. B was his tenacious meekness. What I mean is he had an extraordinary saintly humility of character that would attract so many young people to Christ throughout college life. Several friends converted to the Catholic faith in college and are still practicing. Almost one-third of the Lutheran student body would attend Catholic Mass! Most of the football players were Catholic and upon reflection I am certain that Fr. B was part of the secret to four consecutive national championships! Not one more since he left! He has left a life-long stamp on my soul.

Fr. B's special charism became something so tangible that others could sense it immediately. People have been touched by his homilies, personally in casual exchanges, or in more private conversations. What is stunning to know is that the freedom he blessed others with he, himself, only truly experienced in a trusted and palpable way as he approached his nintieth birthday. After turning ninety, Fr. B has spent more and more time in intimate prayer before the Eucharist in Bellarmine chapel and enjoying freedom and peace like he never knew before. This has become added consolation as he embraces the inevitabilities of aging: a slower gait, a need for hearing aids, more doctor appointments, etc.

As with many of us, Fr. B's pain was mostly private. As a "brother" of St. Ignatius, he chose to focus on consolation that came with the grace and light of his relationship with God, the original community of love, and communion with others. Desolation still pursued him. As forceful as it was, he tried not to be distracted by its dark power. He learned not to hate, but instead to turn his back on it, to reject its grip. This was a practice that led Fr. B into an emotional maturity that saved him. It's a practice we can all learn from him. He chose life so that he could live!

> *I have set before you life and death, the blessing and the curse.*
> *Choose life, then, that you and your descendants may live.*
> (Dt. 30: 19)

CHAPTER 12

The Slow Work of God

Trust in the Slow Work of God

Above all, trust in the slow work of God.

We are quite naturally impatient in everything

to reach the end without delay.

We should like to skip the intermediate stages.

We are impatient of being on the way to something

unknown, something new.

And yet it is the law of all progress that it is made by

passing through some stages of instability—

and that it may take a very long time.

And so I think it is with you;

your ideas mature gradually—let them grow,

let them shape themselves, without undue haste.

Don't try to force them on,

as though you could be today what time

(that is to say, grace and circumstances

acting on your own good will)

will make of you tomorrow.

Only God could say what this new spirit

gradually forming within you will be.

Give Our Lord the benefit of believing

that his hand is leading you,

and accept the anxiety of feeling yourself

in suspense and incomplete.

(Pierre Teilhard de Chardin (1881–1955), French

philosopher, scientist, and Jesuit priest.)

This reflection is testimony to the long slow work of God in Fr. B's long life. In the same way that one sits for a portrait, imagine Fr. B "sitting" as the subject of Teilhard's reflection. Then imagine yourself as the subject. This is how most saints are made ... S-l-o-w-l-y!

The poet and writer anticipated what Fr. B has now come to describe as the slow work of trusting and forgiveness. From early in his life the powerful and aggressive demons of guilt and shame were imprinted on him. His childhood was an emotional paradox of nurturing love from his parents contradicted by the assault of damaging trauma by others. It is only in the last few years of his life that he has felt, for the first time, the true grace and freedom from the oppressive hold guilt has had on him. "Albert, don't beat yourself up. I love you!" is what he hears from God.

Fr. B would say that while most Christians believe in God, they have a much stronger belief that we are separate from God and will never be good enough. This is a pre-Christian pagan mindset that has a hold on every human until they really hear the Good News. Many of us are so pragmatic that we carry a sense of resignation or indifference toward our own character defects or habitual negative behaviors. "That's just me. Take it or leave it. That's who I am." That pragmatism will shield us for a while and protect our fragile egos.

But at some point something needs to change or we will quietly give up hope and die inside. Every part of us needs to open up to the real Good News that we are loveable, and loved, and forgiven. We need to trust that.

Watching our children grow up, the changing love we have for a spouse, less frequent time with friends—often all of this catches up with us in the second half of life and we sense that there is an emptiness that needs to be faced. What once made sense to avoid can't be avoided anymore.

And so a difficult dance begins between the True Self and the coping self. Religion and spirituality either become empty, or we infuse them with new meaning.

Although humility and gratitude are important at every age, at this point in life they become absolutely essential. Unless we give up being the center of the universe and discover a new awe and gratitude for the people in our lives and for God, we may be filled with more and more cynicism and self-disgust. We can numb ourselves with substances or pornography or the attention of new lovers or whatever, but these won't lead us to the truth. Self wants to break through, and so does God, who loves us even though we may not want such intimacy. Being vulnerable is just so painfully hard, but it's necessary and worth it!

We try so hard to "just be normal" in our adolescence and then to become successful and respected adults. Richard Rohr says that the first half of life is all about piety, penitential acts, and moral rectitude, getting everything "right." The second half of life is a school of prayer and surrender to the God who has already saved us. Our task is to allow ourselves to be released from distortions and lies which took hold of us quite naturally in the first half of life. What we thought we knew is just no longer relevant. This "second passage" takes us beyond certitude to a place sometimes of doubt, but eventually a place of mystery.

As our discipleship matures, we can bring our burdens to a loving God for transformation: trauma, guilt, shame, compulsions, addiction, thoughtlessness, judgment, anger, sadness, hurt, confusion, illness, instability, numbness, self-absorption, entitlement, ignorance or fear of the poor and marginalized, lack of faith, lack of hope, lack of love, resignation, grief, despair, cynicism, materialism, secularism, prejudice, etc., etc. *Kenosis* is the traditional Greek term for the emptying out of the false self and the welcoming in of the Risen Christ. This is our heritage, our right, and our destiny. And it's the legacy that Fr. B passionately hopes to leave among us.

Judy Wimberg, retired president of St. Ursula Academy in Cincinnati, offers this reflection:

Al Bischoff has been a guiding light in my life for almost forty years. I ask myself, why has he been so important during all those years through the ups and downs of life. The answer is that he respects his own humanity and has guided me to accept mine, warts and all. Through his guidance and example, I have learned to find the God who loves me in the daily experiences of life.

Years ago he directed me in a private retreat at Augustana College. I started spending the days crossing the Mississippi to sit in a park on the Iowa side. It was a time of crisis in my life and Al quickly saw that crossing the bridge was the essence of the retreat. I have crossed several bridges since that time, and, thanks to him, I have done so without fear (well, not too much fear) knowing that God walks right beside me even though the bridge may be risky. (Al informed me at the conclusion of the retreat that the original bridge was condemned and ready to be torn down. *Right*.)

Sitting before the Lord in the tabernacle or resting in the Lord in his recliner over in Husman Hall, Fr. B allowed God over many years to gradually and tenderly peel away the layers of guilt and shame that had been installed inside of him as an innocent child. He grew able to forgive his culture and Price Hill, to forgive his parents and his perpetrators, to forgive the bishops and the hierarchy, to forgive everyone who wanted him to look more perfect than he was or could ever be. Ultimately, he needed to forgive himself as well. Each of us needs to make that same journey. And we need to bring along every part of us, even our exiles. God wants the Good News to reach every part of our interior "house." Rohr describes the risk and the effort this way. "I am certainly afraid to own—and fully draw upon—that kind of dignity, such deep freedom, and such infinite love." [12]

Aging, he was blessed with a special freedom that submission releases in the disciple. He began submitting not to the law, but to something much, much bigger. This is the blessing of a long life—that we experience the liberation that will be ours in heaven. It's not that our old self is or was bad. It's just too brittle and not big enough to contain the love that is ours to receive. Humility, gratitude, and prayer can transform us from law-abiding people into free and breathing citizens of the kingdom which Jesus came to proclaim. What at first seems like a loss of self turns out to be a discovery of who we were always meant to be. This, finally, is the Self who will live forever.

With each passing year Fr. B let go of the "anxiety of brokenness and incompleteness." He truly came home to rest in the unconditional and intimate love of God, sitting daily before the Blessed Sacrament. He would walk at all hours of the day from his room in Husman Hall the few minutes up the sidewalk to Bellarmine, a walk that used to take five minutes, then later ten or fifteen. There, held in the stillness and the quiet, he soaked up the healing and transforming love of the Risen Christ. For him this is what Thomas Keating describes in contemplative prayer as Divine Therapy:

> Merton—as well as anyone deserving of the title mystic believes that God is always recognizing God's Self in you and cannot not love it. This is God's 'steadfast love' (hesed) with humanity. That part of you has always loved God and always will. You must learn how to consciously abide there. As Meister Eckhart says, 'The eye with which I see God is the same one with which God sees me. My eye and God's eye is one eye, and one sight, and one knowledge, and one love.' There is a part of you that has always said yes to God, and that is the Anointed One, the Christ, the True Self that you already are. William McNamara called contemplative prayer "a long, loving look at the real." Within prayer you quite simply receive and return God's gaze of love. God is recognizing God's Self in you, and you are recognizing yourself in God. Once the two way mirror begins to reflect in both directions, it will gradually move you toward a universal seeing. Once accepted in yourself, the divine image is then seen everywhere else too—and just as gratuitously. [13]

"Grace and freedom like I've never experienced before," Fr. B shares. And it is wonderful and becoming to him. Witnessing this freedom and grace reveals our own destiny as the Saints he has been calling us for so many years. The Risen Christ is not just an external historical fact but also a sacred uprising with the True Christ in each of our souls.

Most of us learned to say no without the deeper joy of yes. Saying no to the false self does not necessarily please God or please anybody, and surely not you. There is too much resentment and self-pity involved in this kind of self-dying ... God tries to first create a joyous yes inside you, far more than any kind of no. Then you have become God's full work of art, and for you, love is stronger than death, and Christ is surely risen in you! The True Self does what it really loves and therefore loves whatever it does. The risen Christ is a great big yes to everything (2 Corinthians 1: 19) even to its own earlier imperfect stages. The final stupendous gift is that your false self has now become your True Self. That is precisely the metamorphosis that we call Resurrection. [14]

As we lose our innocence and engage our brokenness, we come to a place where the false self is revealed for all its disillusioning and misguided efforts. This can be such a desert, such a place of sadness and detachment from all that we thought was reliable. If people just break the coping self but do not welcome the True Self, there is desolation with little consolation. We don't have many safe harbors or constructive forums for people who arrive at this point. They may be shipwrecked on the same island with similar questions and similar needs. Something essential must happen.

This important work leads us to our True Self in Christ. It is, for sure, a struggle between darkness and light, a spiritual warfare that can fatigue and discourage us. If we cooperate with "the slow work of God," as Al has done, then for Catholics, faithfulness to the Eucharist, engagement in a small faith community of like-minded seekers, sitting before and with the Lord with arms and hearts open will slowly accomplish one's ultimate freedom. For others it may be a different path but toward the same end.

One way to approach this intimacy is to start by using one of the oldest prayers in Christianity, a breathing/walking prayer. Breathe in hearing God's voice saying, "I love you, _____ [your name]." As you breathe out, with your own voice say, "I love you, God (or Holy One, or Lord, or Jesus)." Continue repeating this as you breathe in and out. Try it when you are out walking, over and over with each breath. This is great exercise for body and soul.

Other ways within our reach to accomplish this include counseling, therapy, spiritual mentoring, twelve step groups, small faith communities, new or deeper friendships, art, spending time with nature, music, brave examination through study, reflection, and prayer. We would be wise to identify and strengthen our True Self at this point in our life with the intentionality that is required.

Lazarus was dead but Jesus called him forth. We urgently call out for life to flow into our True Self. It's like a soft shell crab as it first emerges from its shell. Realizing it has grown larger, it creates a new home that is bigger and more comfortable. But is this new and expanded container now "me"? Probably not. We are probably going to get bigger still. We stay ready, alert and resilient as we are transformed by an all-loving God. Don't be afraid to look for the Risen Christ every day. He will come. He is already here.

Alexa, play 'My Sweet Lord.'

Fr. B's path was out of childhood trauma. His lifelong submission to God's healing and wholeness reveals a path that we can imitate. Some people give themselves to the service of Christ precisely because of their brokenness and knowing the false self. We see this pattern in the stories of Scripture as people were moved and transformed by the Good News. Jesus restored the marginalized to community and

Fr. B walking with parishioner John Murray toward the Chapel.
Courtesy of Mary Anne Reese

encouraged them to embrace the reign of God which he came to proclaim. This "Good News" set them free. In a very personal way the Risen Christ has set Fr. B free and he has shared that marvelous news with us all these years.

In this process of growth, we may want to reject our former self as if it were "bad" or unrecognizable. Just when this feeling rises up within us, that's when we have to develop compassion for our false self and the remnants of our personality. If we don't, we may end up judging self and others and miss the next stage of our own transformation.

Fr. B was pushed forcefully through these stages, as if driven by the dogs of shame, guilt, and confusion biting at his heels. He has been for many of us an icon for this slow work. He had to find his True Self and cling to it in Christ. The necessity and urgency of a life-saving conversion allowed him to reveal that path with immediacy, simplicity, and clarity. In so doing, he also revealed the *kerygma*, the precious kernel of Good News that illuminates the whole Gospel and the followers of Jesus. Once the soul embraces this growth, one has found the Way, the Truth, and the Life.

CHAPTER 13
Worshipping in Spirit and in Truth

John Baum, XU Class of 1974 and longtime friend, writes:

Even if you didn't know "B" you wanted to figure out how to
know him ... and he made that especially easy. Anyone could
approach him and those that didn't, he often broke down the
barrier. There was no pretense about 'B' ... just a welcome
mat. And once you were in, the world became different
... much better view and clarity using your 'B lenses.'

You always had safe harbor with 'B' ... no matter the problem,
issue, or predicament—he would never judge or scold—just
made you feel better—MOSTLY about yourself. Part of the 'B'
lenses was you got to get a glimpse of yourself through his eyes!
He had that uncanny ability to have you look into his eyes to
see who he saw and oh my God—IT WAS SO GOOD TO SEE!

My favorite gift from "B" is he taught us community. His 7:30 PM
Sunday liturgy was central to so many of our lives ... we would
come for the music, or the homily, or just to simply be with each

other ... the only time in our lives we came early and stayed late!
We were on sacred ground—it could be anywhere—and we just
wanted to be together! We celebrated ... we were real Church.

"B" has been such an influence on my life ... so many of my
friends agree. The 'B experience' didn't stop when you left
Xavier. He has taught us that it can all be real and duplicated.

Fr. B recently had a dream that he had arrived at a beautiful
cathedral to say Mass. The church was packed. He urgently tried to
get ready for Mass. People in the sacristy seemed oblivious to his di-
lemma as he searched for vestments, vessels, bread, and wine. Time
was moving on. As he looked out to see how the congregation was
doing, he now saw that the church was empty—all except for a family
with a child waiting to be baptized. Later he could not even remember whether he had actually used water for the baptism, but he knew
there had been a friendly and grateful exchange with the parents. In
his dream, he told himself that he could go back and pour water later
if needed. As he prepared to leave the church he could not find his
keys, but he did have his wallet, so he knew he had his identity and
the means to get home. Then he woke up.

As Fr. B reflected on this dream with the two of us he realized
that as part of his new freedom in his nineties, he knows that he has
been a faithful priest of the Catholic Church. That which is most important will remain as he heads home to heaven. It's not really about
religion. It's about faith.

Recently, he presided at Bellarmine Chapel on Palm Sunday. His
presence and his preaching were excellent as usual. In his homily he
carefully reviewed the people from John's Gospel whose profound
stories we hear during the final weeks of Lent: the Samaritan

woman at the well, the healing of the man born blind, and the raising of Lazarus from the dead. He recounted how the crowd surrounded Jesus as he entered Jerusalem riding on a donkey.

He remembered with us that the woman at the well was a Samaritan and a sinner. Like all Samaritans she was banned from the temple in Jerusalem. As a known sinner she was banned from joining the other women in public. That's why she was alone at the well and that's how the conversation with Jesus took place. She came alone when no one else would imagine facing the noontime heat. For Jesus, a Jewish man, to speak to her was a violation of law and custom. Among other things they discussed, she asks Jesus where her people should worship. He responds:

> I tell you a time is coming when you will worship the Father neither on this mountain nor in Jerusalem ... But the hour is coming, and is already here, when true worshipers will worship the Father in Spirit and truth. Indeed, the Father is looking for those who will worship him that way. God is Spirit, and those who worship him must worship in Spirit and truth. (Jn. 4: 21; 23–24)

These words confront any of us who think of ourselves as religious people. Rules and rituals have their place, but Spirit and Truth are bigger than doctrine and denomination. A transformed heart is the best worship of all. Living life humbly, gratefully, compassionately is better than any sacrifice. As Fr. B struggled with his own trauma, grief, and confusion over ninety plus years, *Jesus* became his simple proclamation. A good priest has walked among us without judgment, but with humor, grace, compassion, and a capacity for sharing the Good News that we are free and that God loves us!

The single and true purpose of mature religion is to lead you to ever new experiences of your True Self. If religion does not do this, it is junk religion. Every Sacrament, every Bible story, every church service, every sermon, every hymn, every bit of priesthood, ministry, or liturgy is for one purpose: to allow you to experience your True Self—who you are in God and who God is in you—and to live a generous life from that Infinite Source. [15]

If we really hear the Good News it will emancipate us from any bondage in organized religion or in social custom or in tradition. This can be scary for any one of us.

Barbara Rueve Otting's reflection continues:

It was pretty mind-blowing to meet a priest who was much happier to be called "B" than Father. I liked that, too! It conveyed that he was one of us. It was the mid-1960s, Vatican II was stirring winds of change and hope, and it was a time of great excitement in the Church. After centuries of a Church built around the hierarchy, the laity were finally to be recognized as equals, and B embodied this new way of thinking. B has told me in later years about how he and close priest friends would walk for hours and talk about these new ideas and what this new Church would look like. The laity were now being called to greater participation in the liturgy and other aspects of the Church.

At that time, B was the assistant at the Church of the Resurrection in Price Hill, and the "new" Sunday evening liturgies at which he presided were unbelievably alive in the Spirit. This definitely was a new Church! People were hungry to be able to relate to the Mass and hear a positive message of God's love and their own goodness. B's homilies have always nourished my spirit, and it was he who kept me in the Church and led me to a deeper faith. B fed us well, and the congregation stretched out the door. The fire marshals came every Sunday evening to try to keep the Church from becoming dangerously overcrowded. They had their hands full!

Butch Otting reflects:

It is because of B that I am still a member of the Catholic Church. The late '60s were a tumultuous time. I felt that the Church was not directly supporting the civil rights movement, nor was it doing its part to address what I saw as the immorality of the Vietnam war. I was ready to leave the Church. Through his homilies, B helped me and others see the teachings of Jesus and the actions of the Holy Spirit, both in the Church and the world. Maybe they were being suppressed at times in the Church and maybe the institutional church was holding back, but the Spirit was alive in some clergy, in the pews and in the world. We could have an impact by acting within the Church!

In 1969, my fiancé Barbara and I asked B to marry us. He said yes and helped us plan our wedding. Of course, he knew some talented young guitarists who would be happy to provide the music. With Vatican II opening the door to vernacular music, we decided on several contemporary songs. The idea of guitars and "folk" songs had my mother-in-law beside herself. Her daughter was going to have a Hootenanny wedding! It ended up being so moving that afterwards there was quite a buzz about it. B said that one of his priest friends asked, "What did you do at that wedding?" He said that it was the first wedding he knew of where everyone was talking about the wedding Mass and not the reception!

Fr. B's compassion with people was extraordinary. Especially for non-Catholic students at Augustana and at Xavier, the concept of forgiveness was huge! The way in which they were raised in the faith did not strongly hold up the foundational claim of forgiveness of sin and reconciliation with a merciful God. Fr. B convinced them of God's unconditional love because of his love for them.

Fr. B has lived like Jesus in fulfilling the law but shows us how to take one step beyond the law without destroying it. Raised and living his life as an observant and good Catholic, he has always loved those who were not as observant as he. He has understood those who were not Catholic or Christian, and always loved those who identified as sinners and non-believers. This is something that he has communicated to students and all kinds of people throughout his life. Now he, himself, knows and feels this freedom, too. It isn't that religion is not important; it's just that God's love for us is much, much bigger. Maybe we could call Fr. B the "Bishop" of *Original Orthodoxy.* (Google it.) After all, his surname, Bischoff, does mean "bishop."

CHAPTER 14

Our Spirituality is Not Transactional, it's Relational

The schism between the Western Church and the Eastern Church is the schism between the head and the heart. Richard Rohr, Joseph Bernardin, and Thomas Merton helped us "marry" them together. St. Francis tells us that the heart knows best and does not divide people. When the wisdom of the heart speaks there is no good and bad; there is just relationship between God and people, between people and people. In the end love lasts, and Al has kept us focused on love and relationship.

His human stories of his struggles and his empathy for our struggles moved Al to adapt the familiar words of St. Irenaeus that "The glory of God is the human person *struggling* to be fully alive." God does not judge us, but delights in our journey with us, helping us to sort out what is our True Self.

What do people say they love about Fr. B? They love the way they feel when they are with him. Is it Al who makes them feel this way? He has the capacity to call forward the True Self, the childlike part of us, the heart and not the head. Being with him is immediately relational. As he got older, many experienced that their relationship with him was like a grandparent.

We contacted Dan Stelzer of the 2018 XU rugby team to get a quote or a story about Fr. B. When Dan learned that we were writing a book about Fr. B he wrote back and said, "It's my dad, Mike, you should be talking to. He has known Fr. B since he was in college." So we did. He responded immediately with this story:

Father Bischoff arrived at Augustana my freshman year and was the Catholic chaplain for the next six years (1982–1988). He and I hit it off immediately probably because I attended a Jesuit High School, SLU High. His Masses were always packed on Sunday evenings.

I recall him attending several parties at our Fraternity House (Gamma Alpha Beta) where he would bless the keg so that it wouldn't run out! He also put on a retreat for my fraternity my senior year, and it was probably the only event where every single member of the fraternity attended. He really seemed to relate to the issues that college students were going through.

My junior year I struggled with whether I should transfer schools and I had many conversations with him about this. He never tried to make the decision for me but after talking with him I decided to stay and not transfer. That decision led to many other positives in my life (law school for one—he was one of my references at SLU Law and I credit him and my other references with the scholarship I received.)

He has continued to have a strong impact on my life ever since. My family visited him on our way back from vacation one year. After meeting Fr. B, my son, Dan, declared that

he was going to XU. That was 2004 when he was only 8
years old. He did, and he graduated in the class of 2018!

Encountering Fr. B on the way to class took you, in a way, outside
of time and space. It was a sanctuary. Why did this feeling rise up in
us when we were with him? Why did we trust the experience? He was
always uncomfortable with the transactional, but most of us spend
our lives there. We are usually working toward a product, a goal.

Because he was so desperate for affirmation and validation
himself, he was drawn to the "relational." Because he was less interested in "winning" any transaction; because he was unequipped in
some transactional situations and was oppressed by them, he wanted to reinforce that *he was enough* and that *you were enough*. He had a
powerful aptitude to draw everyone into a non-judgmental relational
space. Since he required it for himself, he created it for others so they
could leave their power center behind and enter a more vulnerable
space with him.

That's where Christ meets us, but with a similar intensity, pas-
sion, and insistence. He gets there first, to that space, then invites you
into it immediately or eventually. He could have been an authority
figure. Instead he presents us with a paradox where authority is less
important than the relationship itself. The dualistic nature of transactional thinking doesn't work anymore.

In many ways, a university environment has to be transactional.
People are being measured against established benchmarks to au-
thenticate their academic achievements. Al's presence was not about
academic achievement on campus. Living in the dorm, eating in the
cafeteria, walking on the mall—these were all about the relational.
He was allowed by the university to represent this precious realm.
He is that authentic part of the institution that delights in each and

every individual completely apart from their productivity. In our culture this is a rare gift.

It was not that he was anti-intellectual. Actually, some who were highly intellectual misunderstood him, and it hurt. But he accepted that judgment instead of foregoing a relational, non-dual way of being with each of us. It was his unique way of being a Jesuit.

In the later years of his ministry, he believed that he had been sent, not as a teacher, but as a pastor. Like Pope Francis, he would say, "If you don't smell like the sheep, you're not a very good pastor!" Al wanted to smell like the sheep he loved, even the freshman men in Husman Hall, where the predominant scents were sweat, testosterone, and deodorant!

What he created was a kind of "liminal" space. It was temporary and short-lived, but it felt very good.

CHAPTER 15

How Fr. B Lived Ignatian Spirituality's: Cura Personalis

(Note to the reader: *Cura personalis* is Latin for "personal care," or more broadly, "individualized attention to the needs of the other, distinct respect for his or her unique circumstances and concerns, an appropriate appreciation for his or her particular gifts and insights." This quality is included in descriptions of Ignatian spirituality.)

Here's a letter written to Fr. B from Marcus Mescher, XU theology faculty, on October 30, 2017:

Dear Fr. B,

I just came from an event that we organized, "Why Celebrate LGBTQ Month at Xavier University?" It was designed to give students a space to process what we risk with such events—and what we risk if we don't celebrate them. I heard from a number of students who had some strong feelings about this topic, but the most meaningful comment of the night came from the co-president of the LGBTQ Alliance, who shared a story from their first meeting of the year: when you came to their meeting up in the third floor of the GSC and said, "Hello Saints. I just want to say I love you and God loves you just as you are." The student was tearful in sharing how much this meant to him (even as someone who identifies as a former Catholic and current agnostic), which generated a lot of other students to agree. I just wanted to write to you to say thank you for your ministry of presence, accompaniment, and support for our students. The way you incarnate "Cura Personalis" means more than you'll know!

Gratefully,

Marcus Mescher Ph.D.

Assistant professor of Christian ethics, Xavier University

In the journal *Jesuit Higher Education,* 3(2): 6–20 (2014), author Fr. Barton T. Geger, S.J., published *"Cura Personalis: Some Ignatian Inspirations."* Here is an excerpt:

In the service of *cura personalis,* the writings of Ignatius and early Jesuits contain yet another gem, and one that bears numerous connections to other Jesuit values. It is the art of 'spiritual conversation.' Shortly after his spiritual conversion at Castle Loyola, Ignatius began to recognize that engaging people in relatively informal, spontaneous, one-on-one conversations about God, faith, and best practices in the spiritual life was a powerful means to edify both them and him. Such conversations, by their nature, circled around the particular concerns and desires of Ignatius's interlocutors and, as a result, they could be much more effective than a sermon, lecture, or book. What is more, since they could be practiced by anyone, anywhere, Ignatius could make a conscious ministry of it without the need to be ordained a priest or to possess a theology degree (both of which were still fifteen years away). [16]

What Ignatius discovered through the circumstances of his daily life, Fr. B practiced instinctively. His own deep desire for God connected him in simple conversation and friendship with the same desire for God he recognized in each one of us. There was no chance encounter. Every person's story led to a revelation of God's marvelous love. Fr. B did that for us. We can do that for one another.

In the very early spring each year at XU a new group of students begins to prepare for the sacrament of Confirmation. One of the first

Al praying for healing with a parishioner during Bellarmine Chapel all-parish Mass March 10, 2019.
Courtesy of Rich Sofranko

sessions was always a "Q and A" with Fr. B, intentionally scheduled so that the students could meet him. One year there was a young man in the group whose mother and fiancée encouraged him to come. He was attending the sessions in good faith but not quite owning the decision himself. He said that every time he got near a church or people talking about faith, he felt lots of anxiety. It was suggested that he talk with Fr. B. An open conversation turned into confession, which turned into an experience of God's unconditional love, leading this young man into a new sense of freedom. He was able to confidently choose Confirmation for himself.

Sr. Rose Anne Fleming, SNDdeN, Special assistant to the president and faculty athletic advisor, reflects:

One of my fondest memories of Father B occurred in Xavier's Fenwick Cafeteria. A friend, Sr. Jane Roberts, and I would meet there just before noon every Sunday for brunch. At first we were surprised, as we walked in, to hear Fr. B call, 'Hey Jane, Rose Ann, come sit with me.' We signaled that we would join. Those breakfasts taught us two things: One was what Ignatius meant by *Cura Personalis*; the other was how Fr. B engaged students.

Generally, our conversation began with his asking to share the homily that he was developing for the 4:00 PM student Mass. In his humility, he wanted to know what we thought about the homily. His words were Gospel-centered in phrases that the students could comprehend and always ended with a suggestion of how they could apply the Good News to their own lives. As we listened to him, it was easy to understand the words of Christ, "I am with you always … " two thousand years later through Fr. B speaking to these Xavier students.

As we continued talking, he would wave his hand and call 'Hey Saint, come here, I want to introduce you' to students who were always pleased to be recognized by him. Each 'Saint' would quickly come to the table so Fr. B could ask for the latest news about home or classes. Then he would introduce Sr. Jane and me, and repeat this process three to four times during breakfast. We knew the real reason he was sitting in the middle of the cafeteria.

He wanted every student to know how important they were, that Xavier was their "family" away from home, and that they belonged to all of us who had gathered for brunch that morning. Over the two-year period when Jane and I met on Sunday mornings with Al, we were drawn into this mission of his to make every student know that she or he was holy, loved by God (why else call him Saint!), and that Fr. B was there for him or her. Indeed this clearly was *Cura Personalis* in action, and we were very grateful to be witnesses.

Thank you, Fr. B!

Among the many people who have experienced this *cura personalis*, this distinct respect of one's circumstances, are a number of men who have left the priesthood over the years. Fr. B has sought them out with compassion as a true and trusted brother and friend.

CHAPTER 16

Prayer and Transformation

How does Fr. B pray? How do I want to pray?

He says that when he wakes up each morning he sits on the edge of the bed, blesses himself in the name of the Father and of the Son and of the Holy Spirit. Then he asks God, "What do you want me to do today?" and "Lord, increase my faith!"

Jesuits learn early in their formation to pray the daily Examen. (See Appendix C.) This simple prayer flows from sitting in God's presence, to being filled with gratitude, to reviewing the day before and discovering God's presence there, to asking forgiveness, to responding to God's invitation to this new day. Fr. B will say that the Examen has become so familiar to him that the steps are no longer required. When he sits in prayer the Spirit immediately draws him into God's loving presence and through it into a sense of enormous deep gratitude. "How can I welcome Christ into my heart and my home?"

The hallmarks of the true sacred self are humility, gratitude, and service. Henri Nouwen wrote, "In the past I always thought of gratitude as a spontaneous response to the awareness of gifts received, but now I realize that gratitude can also be lived as a discipline. The discipline of gratitude is an explicit effort to acknowledge that all I am and have is given to me as a gift of Love."

As is the practice of priests, Fr. B daily prays the Divine Office or "The Prayer of the Church," followed by the rosary "for all those I have promised to pray for."

Fr. B presiding at First Communion Mass at Bellarmine Chapel April 6, 2008.
Courtesy of Rich Sofranko

"The Eucharist is the source and the summit of the Christian life."(#1326) [17] For Fr. B celebrating the Eucharist is his daily bread within a loving community—it's everything! Even when he is not presiding, he joins students and parish members who have gathered in the pews and prays right alongside them as the Body of Christ.

When he does preside, after Communion he sits and invites us, "Now let's close our eyes and talk to Jesus and tell him what's going on." And then, with the final dismissal, he encourages us, "Now go in peace and take good care of one another."

Fr. B shared this example of how God can use our imaginations in prayer. "A couple of years ago when I was praying, I invited my mother and father and sister to come and be with me when I pray. It was a way for me to have the close family now which I did not always have growing up."

Another essential Jesuit practice is praying The Spiritual Exercises of St. Ignatius. During the Third Week the prayer leads one into reflecting on the suffering and death of Jesus. This meditation over many years remained often too personal and too painful, pulling Fr. B into a deep depression. It was finally, at the age of ninety-two, during his summer retreat that he was able to complete The Spiritual Exercises on his own, without the accompaniment of a spiritual director. After years of praying and working through his own suffering, he had a newfound freedom and healing that allowed him to move through the Third Week and into the Fourth Week. Finally, he was able to savor the joy and consolation of the Risen Lord, the gift that Ignatius teaches that God always intended.

During Lent of 2019, one day when Fr. B was deep in prayer, he had an image of his family gathered to say the rosary, a practice they shared often. This time, as he imagined the scene, Al saw the face of the priest who had sexually abused him many years before. This time, all these years later, his response was not to feel fear or anger or even sadness. This time, he invited the priest to join his family and pray the rosary together. "The Saints are distinguished by a spirit of prayer and a need for communion with God." (#147) [18]

When we surrender into prayer, our hearts can be transformed. *Metanoia!*

Fr. B, in good company with Pope Francis, encourages us into the most essential prayer of all, just sitting in the loving presence of God. As Teresa of Avila describes, "having a conversation with the one who we know loves us." "I would insist that this is true not only for a privileged few, but for all of us." (#149) [19]

In May of 2019, Fr. B moved out of his home of many years in the residence hall and into the Jesuit residence on campus. Just a few weeks later he went out to Milford for his scheduled retreat. Even after ninety-two years of living and retreating this priest still received just the gifts his heart and soul needed from his beloved God.

There were several epiphanies. Al's prayer took him back to his first love for Lois in high school. He realized that the part of himself who wanted to marry her was angry with the part of himself who wanted to be a priest. The part of himself who loved her but could not be with her had remained depressed for much of his life.

His prayer also led him to recall people over the years whom he felt he had disappointed or failed. God told him to pray for them. He did, and he was released from lifelong burden he had been carrying.

He had a dream about a young uptight, anxious, conforming priest who knelt down in front of him, asking for his blessing. Al realized the young priest was himself asking for God's blessing, particularly on the years of his young ministry at Elder High School.

Finally, he had an experience of God holding an umbrella and walking with him through the different parts of his life, showing how he had protected Al from things he could not have handled, or would not have been good at dealing with, or that would have greatly disturbed him. God showed him clearly and providentially how each time he had moved Al on to a new ministry out of protection and love.

Our hearts are restless until they rest in you, Oh, Lord.

—St. Augustine

Prayer of Final Surrender

by Pierre Teilhard de Chardin

When my hour comes, O God,

grant that I may recognize you

under the species of each alien or hostile force

that seems bent upon

destroying or uprooting me.

When the signs of age begin to mark my body (and

still more when they touch my mind);

when the ill that is to diminish me or carry me

off strikes from without or is born within me;

when the painful moment comes

in which I suddenly awaken to the fact that I am ill or growing old;

and above all at that last moment when I feel I am losing

hold of myself and am absolutely passive within the hands of

the great unknown forces that have formed me;

in all those dark moments, O God, grant that

I may understand that it is you

(provided only my faith is strong enough) who are painfully

parting the fibers of my being in order to penetrate to the very

marrow of my substance and bear me away within yourself.

Teach me to know my death

as an act of communion with you.

—The Divine Milieu

CHAPTER 17

The Communion of Saints

Tapestry of the saints at the Cathedral of Our Lady of the Angels, Los Angeles.
Courtesy of Jane Myers

We chose to include these extraordinary images of saints created for the Cathedral of Our Lady of the Angels in Los Angeles. The artist's inspiration for these tapestries brilliantly captures the essential message we are writing to convey—*we are all Saints!*

Here is an excerpt from the website. Read the full description about these marvelous tapestries at *www.olacathedral.org/cathedral/art/tapestries.html.*

The tapestries were created by artist John Nava ... the most prominent is the Communion of Saints along the south and north walls of the nave. Twenty-five fresco-like tapestries depict 135 saints and blesseds from around the world, including holy men and women of North America canonized by the Church. Twelve untitled figures, including children of all ages, represent the many anonymous holy people in our midst.
All the figures direct our eyes to the light of the great Cross-window above the Altar where the Eucharist is celebrated.

Nava combined digital imaging and "Old Master" methods in creating the saints for the tapestries. He constructed figures from multiple studies, combined drawn and painted elements, had costumes made when needed and even drafted family members to serve as models on occasion. He wanted the figures to look like people we know now, and did not use a highly stylized form to depict the saints. Nava's desire is that people identify and see that "a saint could look like me."

The Communion of Saints consists of females and males of all ages, races, occupations and vocations the world over. Saints from the Renaissance are intermingled with people from the 1st century and the 20th century. [20]

For Al's ninetieth birthday in 2017, the *XU News* reported that he was "still spry, jovial and wise at ninety years old!" The children of our Bellarmine parish faith formation made cards for Fr. B. The card from the 5th and 6th graders was personally signed, "Happy Birthday from your Saints, St. Patrick, St. Rachel, St. Nola, St. Brendan, St. Mitchell, St. Caitie ... " They know who the saints are because of Fr. B!

Fr. B with First Communion children at Bellarmine Chapel April 6, 2008.
Courtesy of Rich Sofranko

Continuing with the riches of "Rejoice and Be Glad" Pope Francis offers us yet another compelling image of sainthood:

> Each Saint is a mission, planned by the Father to reflect and embody, at a specific moment in history, a certain aspect of the Gospel ... That mission has its fullest meaning in Christ, and can only be understood through him. It consists in uniting ourselves to the Lord's death and resurrection in a unique and personal way, constantly dying and rising anew with him. Every Saint is a message which the Holy Spirit takes from the riches of Jesus Christ and gives to his people. (#19–21) [21]

Dan Hartnett, S.J., former pastor of Bellarmine Chapel, describes how Fr. B called us all to the Communion of Saints.

As soon as you come into Al's view, he typically states in a loud, sincere voice: 'Saint, it is so good to see you!' Not only do these words have the immediate effect of making you feel appreciated but, by using the salutation 'saint,' Al reminds people that the fire of holiness is something we carry within. A truth we all-too-often forget or neglect.

Then, right after shaking your hand, Al promptly lets you know the he has a story to share. Such stories typically combine humor with deep wisdom. Much like Jesus who usually spoke in parables, Al realizes that holiness cannot be contained in a concept; it is more intelligible and best communicated via story.

Most interestingly, Al employs the term 'saint,' not only in his one-on-one interactions, but also when addressing a large group or assembly. By so doing, he reminds us that we belong to the 'communion of saints.' We are called to grow in holiness together; it is not a competition but rather a shared vocation.

Francis's words affirm this description. "The powerful witness of the Saints is revealed in their lives, shaped by the Beatitudes and the criterion of the final judgment. Jesus' words are few and straightforward, yet practical and valid for everyone, for Christianity is meant above all to be put into practice." (#109) [22]

CHAPTER 18

The Jesuit Challenge to Serve Others

The lesson Fr. B has taught us with his life is that we do not need to earn heaven. We do not work or serve or suffer to make God love us. That is a false religion. The Good News is that God loves us, every cell and fiber of our being. We share DNA with Jesus, God's beloved son. The risen Christ infiltrates us, body and soul. Our destiny is heaven already claimed for us. That has already been taken care of. We give ourselves to life and to each other by responding full-heartedly in love and as God loves.

Many prophets and holy people of the Hebrew Scriptures died for their faith and their faithfulness to God. Many thousands of unnamed Hebrews died in Egypt under the Pharaoh. Millions of Jews died in the Holocaust. At this very moment, men and women are being tortured and even crucified and beheaded in the Middle East. So many children of God have been persecuted and have died at the hands of oppressors from ancient Israel to this very moment in history. We are, like God, heartbroken for suffering humanity.

This is the history we must never forget. Only slightly less than being martyred, the plight of millions of refugees and the obscene income inequality in our own country and throughout the world have scandalized us all from pope to presidential candidates. We are all complicit in the international structures that allow this to continue. We know that genocide and ethnic cleansing continue to afflict many parts of the world. We know that there are more slaves now than ever before in history through sex trade and other outrageous acts by gangs and aggressors throughout the world.

Innocent and defenseless children and adults are being exploited, neglected, abandoned, tortured, and murdered on almost every continent. Wars, threats of war, ancient tribal struggles, nationalism, the hoarding of wealth, ignorance, lack of access to education and resources, and many other forces, old and new, contribute to the suffering and death of our human brothers and sisters throughout the world. The privileged and the powerful collude directly or indirectly in these injustices and horrors.

Fr. B is not naïve about human sin and suffering. He calls us to some accountability whether we grew up in Price Hill or the Midwest suburbs or other enclaves of safety and security. We are, in many ways, the privileged and the powerful. The Good News that Fr. B has always proclaimed with such simple freshness is a Gospel of joy, peace, and harmony. He has always urgently reassured us that we are "Saints" and that we are claimed by a loving God.

John the Baptist and Jesus, the children of Elizabeth and Mary, were cousins who both had been baptized by water and the Holy Spirit. They were Jewish men of great strength and great faith. We can also count them as the first martyrs of the New Covenant between God and the Saints. Jesus and his twelve apostles, Mary, and hundreds of disciples were given the special grace from God to see and to understand and to proclaim the New Creation, the Reign of God. In that way, Jesus was the new Adam, the firstborn human of the New Creation. He walked among the poor and marginalized. He was not rich. He had no earthly power. He did not become a priest of his religion. He did not seek status in Jerusalem or in the Temple. Instead, he spoke truth to power and comforted the outcast and the afflicted.

Jesus healed many poor widows, orphans, lepers, those possessed by frightening afflictions and demons. He not only healed them, but he restored them to relationship and to community. Those who were disgusting and untouchable were welcomed by him with open arms and given a status in the New Creation that was unassailable by the powerful and privileged. Their confidence and joy became so strong that they could tolerate even more suffering and rejection, even martyrdom. It's an amazing story, and we are part of that legacy. This is why stories of Saints are the heritage we have a right to claim.

Those of us who have been around for a while have witnessed recent martyrs and Saints of international reputation. Ghandi, Martin Luther King, Archbishop Oscar Romero, the four women who served in El Salvador, the Jesuits at the University of Central America, Brother Roger of Taizé, people of faith throughout the world. More have died for the Christian faith in the last 50 years than in all of the previous 2000 years. Hindus, Muslims, Jews, Buddhists and faithful followers of just about every religion in the world have also been systematically persecuted, tortured, and killed for their devotion. Jesus came to celebrate hope, faith, and love among humanity, but he deliberately embraced his cross as both priest and victim to show his solidarity with suffering humanity, then and now.

We must choose to either collude with the rich and powerful or serve the poor and marginalized of the world. It is not an option to remain an innocent bystander. The proclamation of the Reign of God keeps getting co-opted by the powerful. Solidarity with the poor and marginalized is the only congruent way toward universal love. We are challenged to live a solidarity with God's suffering people everywhere, which includes our own neighborhoods.

So, who are "God's people?" Fr. B has lived into his nineties, and we are alive right now. How are we to live in the breach between the privileged/powerful and the masses of people who are suffering on the other side? How can we be consoled by our own health and safety unless we work for the New Reign of justice, mercy, and peace? The most compelling way he showed us is to live it one loving relationship at a time.

Matthew Shannon, class of 2019, Army ROTC cadet, president, XU HR Club writes:

Father B to me is the definition of what every Catholic should be. He truly loves and serves everyone. He makes you feel valued and appreciated no matter what you may have going on that day. I remember the first time I met Father B when he referred to me as a Saint. Saint meaning a person who has "an exceptional degree of holiness, or closeness to God." Despite whatever I was going through, hearing Father B call me a Saint always made me feel valued, special and cared for.

Over the years, I've grown even closer to Father B. whether it's been through eating lunch in the "caf;" or one of our favorites, Quatman's Café; grabbing Graeter's, attending ROTC Events, Church or just crossing each other's paths. We talk about everything: How our days are going, Xavier Basketball, ROTC, homilies, high school memories, our friends, family and our faith. There is never a dull experience or conversation with Father B.

Here's a favorite memory. We were at Xavier's Annual ROTC Military Ball when I went to get myself and my girlfriend a drink at the bar. I went to pay for the two drinks with a debit card to find out that the bar was cash only. Who came to the rescue? Fr. B, of course. He spotted me some cash to pay for the drinks. Ok, great, Father paid for your drink at a bar Matt, so where are you going with this story, you may be asking.

The next morning I ran into Fr. B at the caf and we were catching up on the night before. I thanked him again for lending me money for the drinks, then went on to say I was going to an ATM nearby to pay him back. He was quick to decline. I didn't accept that as an option, and insisted I would be back with the money. Fr. B quickly grabbed my hand. "Matt, the best way you can pay me back is by doing a good deed for another person. That means more to me than the money."

Xavier is truly blessed and fortunate to have Father B on campus. I am also blessed and fortunate to have shared great experiences with him. As I near the end of my college career at Xavier, Father B stands out as a person who has had one of the biggest impacts on me to become the man I am today. He will continue to be the caring, loving and serving Catholic man that he is every day. He'll continue to call everyone he meets "Saint." In the end everyone who has had the opportunity to know who Father B truly is, will know and understand who the real Saint is.

Those who have died suffering for goodness are called the "red martyrs" because of the blood they have shed. Celtic spirituality and Catholic Christian tradition understand what is known as "white martyrdom." This is a phenomenon that describes those who leave the simple comforts of their childhood to pursue education and service among their suffering brothers and sisters. Sometimes this was in a life of prayer embracing a cell in a monastery, consciously suffering with and praying with others less fortunate. Sometimes this meant responding to a call to serve.

We know and admire teachers, first responders, those who work closely with diseased or otherwise afflicted individuals, parents who take on the burden of infant care and child raising, people who every day make career or investment or philanthropic decisions inspired by a sense of justice or mercy, those caring for the elderly and the dying, or even small daily acts of selfless love. These are the Saints! These are the people of God no matter what race or religion, no matter what gender, status, privilege, or power. These are the good, gathered everywhere in conscious relationships of hope and encouragement and love. We are all familiar with how St. Francis said it best, "Preach the Gospel at all times. If necessary, use words."

Fr. B, although hounded by his own suffering, darkness, and despair, embraced the light and joy, and even laughter, in compassionate union with others. Students from every diverse race and religion and national origin all recognize in him a true companion. Most exquisitely, he gives them that special respect that comes from actually enjoying them and delighting in them, drawing them into a moment of levity and laughter, acceptance, and joy. Perhaps you have been directly touched in this way if you know him. That part of us that resonates with this compassion is the part of us he calls "Saint."

There are countless ways that each of us has deferred to others, making decisions to love against all odds. Every time we do that we open a door into the reign of God. We pass through that door and bring others with us. We cross a line and stand up for suffering humanity, and that changes everything. It is a forever covenant. Even when we fail to love we are forgiven by the author of this pact with humanity.

Al praying with parishioners at Bellarmine Chapel all-parish Mass March 10, 2019.
Courtesy of Rich Sofranko

Darkness and death are already disappearing even if it does not seem so. The victory has already been won. This is the meaning of Fr. B's witness, his life and legacy, and this is the meaning of "Hello Saints!"

Fr. B has always loved and delighted in witnessing each Saint's journey. "What a joy!" That special grace of appreciation lifted him out of the darkness of his own journey, and he meets with us on higher ground. We, too, are lifted up and God is glorified in the process, in this exchange. This is why his acclamation feels so special and powerful. It is based in relationship and in Jesus.

As a man of faith, as a priest, and as a Jesuit, we of course know what he stands for. But we need no lengthy intellectual analysis when he lifts us up as one of his Saints. "Hello Saints!" is a proclamation of Good News, a bold defiance of the darkness and a powerful blessing and prayer. If this were not so, we would not have written this, and you would not be reading it. His words proclaim our truth.

Watch an interview with Al Bischoff, S.J., on youtube: *"How I Live the Mission" (of Xavier University.) https://www.xavier.edu/mission-identity/programs/Father-Al-Bischoff,-SJ.cfm produced by the Center for Mission and Identity, Xavier University.*

CHAPTER 19
What Difference Does it Make?

John Barber, XU Class of 2012, recalls:

My very first impression of Fr. B was at orientation (PREP) before freshman year. He gave a speech to us and it was so timely for me personally that I will never forget the end, "Saints, no matter what happens always remember that God loves you." I am powerfully reminded of this every time I see him.

My freshman year at XU (08–09) was tough. I came from a very small rural town in central Kentucky where I stood out. At Xavier I was challenged with a new city, culture, and curriculum. I knew no one and everything was new to me.

I started going to daily Mass because it was the one thing that was nearly the same as what I was used to at home, so it gave me comfort. That's where I met Fr. B. After a long hard fall semester I was at the 8:00 AM Mass before my last final before heading home for Christmas break. At the end of Mass Fr. B turned to me among the small crowd of 9 or 10 who were not students. He said "Saint, good luck on your finals and enjoy Christmas with your family." My relationship with Fr. B aside, that moment reassured me why I chose Xavier. I wanted to be at a faith-based school where people cared about me. He is an irreplaceable asset to XU in that sense. I knew Fr. B was "famous" and having him speaking personally to me made me feel valued. As our relationship grew, he could make me feel as at home as any hug from my mom, which is something most college freshman long for but never admit.

After we interacted a few more times he asked me to coordinate the 4:00 PM student Mass for him, which I did from sophomore through senior year. I basically made sure the logistics were taken care of (lectors, Eucharistic ministers, etc.) so he could focus on the liturgy. Fr. B was so calming to others, yet it was funny to know how much he worried about small things related to the 4:00 PM Mass. He likes to tell this story: he came to me one Sunday around 3:50 PM in a small panic about whether we had enough lectors for Mass. I took him by the hand and said "come with me" and I led him to the small chapel where he liked to pray before Mass. I said "sit here and I'll come get you when we need you." He chuckled, but actually really appreciated the reassurance and our trust grew that day.

In recent years Fr. B had a brief phase where he admitted to me he had been reflecting on his life and wondering how much of an impact he had really made. (It might seem crazy to you and me, but I can understand where at that age you just question life from time to time.) At any rate, it gave me a sense of urgency to show him my appreciation. I was able to start a scholarship in his name at Elder High School. He had shared many stories about his fondness for teaching there earlier in his life.

We held a reunion and fundraiser at Cintas in fall 2015 for this where he was able to see friends from 40+ years ago. That was the best part. In a perfect Fr. B moment he told me before the event (exclusive/invitation-only/fee per plate) that if no one showed up he wanted me to know how much he appreciated the gesture. Of course, hundreds of people came, from as far away as Florida. The scholarship was really just a nice bonus for the appreciation party we were able to throw him. This bonus amounted to $75,000!

So, what difference does Fr. B's life make? The difference it makes is the Kingdom, the Reign of God! He has accompanied the people of God into this way of life. As Paul says, he has committed his life to serving the Saints, never having met anyone who is not one. His love for humanity and zeal for the Kingdom are the seamless garment he has worn, recognized by each of us, as if with a special sixth sense.

Many of us have been accompanied in our marriages by Fr B. He says:

When I returned to Xavier in 1998, a great part of my work in the parish was preparing couples for marriage. I knew them as a student, in the residence halls or from the 4:00 PM Mass. I may have known them growing up in their family at Bellarmine Chapel. It's important to see where God is in their life and prepare them for this sacrament. Many of the couples at Bellarmine choose me because there's a relationship.

I put an average of seven hours into preparing each marriage, and I really think about the conversations we have. They're on my mind and in my prayers, and in some sense I fall in love with them and feel committed to them because they're part of my prayer life. I see marriage as a crucial point in their life of faith. I say to the couple, 'It's a commitment in good times and bad.' That's what love is. I had a couple who wanted to get married in a park because they weren't sure if they were still Catholic. I had known them as students. So I said, "let's talk about that." In the end they came to me and decided they were Catholic at the core and they wanted a wedding in the church.

In a July 2015 article, "Proud to Be a Cafeteria Catholic" in the journal *Parish Life*, author Isabella R. Moyer writes the following. As she speaks of Pope Francis, think also of Fr. B:

The recent Synod on the family discussed the concept of graduality, which acknowledges that we are all on a path to wholeness and holiness. None of us is perfect. As we hope for compassion for our own imperfections, we are also called to offer the same compassion to others. If we focus only on seeking the sinfulness in others, we will not see the goodness that is present in them.

Gone are the days of the blind, unquestioning obedience. Gone are the days of conversion by fear. Gone are the days of forcing and enforcing beliefs through militant apologetics with the expectation that doctrinal arguments can be ended with a simple catechism quote.

Evangelization today requires a real dialogue, a sharing that seeks to build on the existing good that unites us while trying to better understand that which divides us. It requires speaking from the head and the heart. The new evangelization calls for a new style of conversation in our church. If we want a model of what this looks like, we need only look to our pope.

Francis speaks first and foremost from his heart to the hearts of others. He knows that the heart is the privileged depository for true conversion. He speaks of faith less in doctrinal terms of the mind and more in practical works of our hands. He is not afraid to denounce, but he saves his harshest condemnations for those who allow legalities to overshadow compassion or who seek personal glory and comfort before the good of others.

Last July, Pope Francis made headlines for joining Vatican workers for lunch in their cafeteria. The cafeteria is a beautiful symbol of what our church community could be like. The church should not be like an elitist restaurant with high-minded hosts zealously guarding the guest list. Invitations to dine should not depend on who we are or who we know. We should not be asked to leave because our manners, dress, or food preferences do not hold up to some exclusive club rules.

We should be a church more like a cafeteria, offering a welcome sense of hospitality to all who seek spiritual nourishment, community, and respite from their worries and labors. But please, let's not ruin the meal by judging what others have on their trays. [23]

It's amusing that the cafeteria was a place where many of us regularly ran into Fr. B! He subscribed to this notion of "graduality" long before it became popular. We are all on a path; none of us is perfect; the heart is the true depository for faith. Let us celebrate each other's goodness, for we are all Saints.

This means that hope is real. Cynicism and judgment must surrender to faith, hope, and love. How is it that religion has so often missed the point? Good News is only good! There is no "but" after it. It's either real or it isn't. If I'm a Christian I proclaim the Good News and the reign of God. It's real in me and in you and in everyone. I can receive the greeting "Hello Saints," and I can trust that it's real. I can look at everyone else and allow my heart to say "Hello Saint" to each person, no matter their circumstances, beliefs, trauma, or sins. As Christians we believe it is real and already accomplished. Our job is to live as if we are celebrating that fact and uncovering that truth in the world around us!

CHAPTER 20

The Risen Christ

Honoring Fr. B, we have tried to be as inclusive as possible in talking about the Saints. Our global village has challenged all of us to embrace a more diverse pluralistic society in our work, in our travel, in recreation, in our churches, in our neighborhoods, and in our families. The news, the complex economics of the world, the internet, all affect us on a daily basis and challenge us to try to understand other people and other cultures and far-reaching geopolitical issues. Exhausting! But the good thing is that we no longer believe that any of us has a monopoly on the truth, values, or best practices. This is not "relativism," and this goes beyond tolerance. This is humility, gratitude, and respect. We all have been created in the image and likeness of God.

Fr. B challenges us to a non-judgmental acceptance of the varieties of alternative lifestyles. Many people have moved from enforcing historical ethnic moralities and norms to a kind of pragmatic non-judgmental acceptance. Some are quick to point out that this leads to a creeping moral relativism or secular materialism as a new common creed throughout western society and the world. Some wish to close ranks and accept what they believe is a morally pure if smaller "People of God." Some have adopted a fortress mentality, us vs. them. Those who can't quite sign on for this militancy, those who refuse to submit to this kind of protectionism, find themselves struggling to decide what, if anything, they should commit to, either for themselves, for their children, or with others.

The church participated in this shifting milieu when Pope John XXIII convened the Second Vatican Council. He proclaimed *aggiornamento* and threw open the doors of the church to dialogue and interface with the modern world. Ever since that process was set in motion, Catholic popes and hierarchy have vacillated between two identities, one as custodians and stewards of morality and doctrine, the other as pastoral leaders with dispositions of non-judgment and mercy.

One of the key documents of Vatican II, the "Declaration on Religious Freedom," took a giant step forward in asserting the primacy of individual conscience. This shifted the burden of education, research, and formation from a select caste of priests and teachers and placed it on the individual, him- or herself. With this incredible shift the church became a guide and resource instead of ruler, prophet and witness instead of authority.

Once that genie of religious liberty and individual conscience was out of the bottle that had contained it for almost 2000 years, it could not be returned. Catholics and Protestants came closer together by their joint faith in the individual and a strengthened belief in the guidance of the Holy Spirit. This has been underestimated as perhaps the biggest and boldest moment in the history of organized religion. The age of the internet has contributed by creating rapid democratization of information, thought, and choice.

Catholics by the millions began to assert their own valid discernment of what is right and wrong, especially captured in the growing acceptance of artificial birth control. Conservatives had predicted a domino collapse of morality with respect to the sanctity of marriage and the sanctity of life. Some would say this predicted free-fall is exactly what has happened.

Civil Rights, the women's movement, the choice movement, gender civil rights, along with many other currents, have delivered us into a world of selective moral norms for oneself and unprecedented tolerance toward the choices of others. So, is religion dying? Less than 50% of Catholics attend Mass every Sunday, contrasted with over 90% fifty years ago. Churches and schools have closed and been sold. Beloved parishes built by immigrant grandparents now operate under new management as recording studios, breweries, wedding venues, restaurants, museums, and condos.

Does it make any sense to look at the life and legacy of an old priest, an old Jesuit? Beloved as he is, how can the life of an old celibate man who lives in a dorm with 300 college freshmen have anything to say to us? Doesn't he represent a dying Church and culture? What possible relevance can there be? What transfer of learning can come from his life to the complexity of contemporary families and individuals?

You must not think so since you are still reading. We invite you to persist in reflecting on his relevance and his witness. We continue to ponder this mystery with you.

The kernel of truth, the essential significance at least for us who are Christian, is that Fr. B has known and walked with the Risen Christ. Indirectly, but persistently, he invites us to always be looking for the Risen Christ in our own heart, our own mind, our own daily experience. The imprint of the human and divine Christ is real and powerful. Let's search the parts of ourselves, the quiet and holy places within. Let's search every room until we find the Risen Christ.

Let's look into our own moments of good will, loving acts, our own hope, faith, and love. Let's look deeply into our own joy, into gentle laughter, into our moments of awe and wonder, and there we will find the Risen Christ. If we have this attitude of faithful expectation, we will make this extraordinary and life-changing discovery.

And, as we look at each person we meet today, and especially if we do so with open expectation, we may see the Risen Christ. Let's look into the lives of suffering humanity in ourselves, in our family, neighborhood, co-workers, in our city; and let's find in that suffering the beginnings of transformation.

Fr. B showed us all how to be surprised and delighted when we are rewarded by finding the Risen Christ. The amazing thing is that he so easily saw the Risen Christ in us! "Of course," he would say. His instinctive response is not just to *look at Christ* but

Students from the 4:00 PM Mass community gave this cap to Fr. B at the end of the spring semester 2019.
Courtesy of Jane Myers

to feel his joy and *run to him*. If imagining this is too much for us, that's O.K. Just keep pondering and trying to be open to it. It's a mystery. Remember, this book is about *us*.

If we embrace this consciously and if we celebrate this with others, both casually and among intentional gathered communities, it will be easier to see and we will know how to behave. We will know how to navigate through this confusing and changing world. We will know how to act with integrity and respect and humility and gratitude, and we will know how to pray. If we keep reaching for and witnessing the Risen Christ, every breath we take is in union with Christ. Our hands and our words and our decisions will be the hands and words and decisions of the Risen Christ. This will become more and more and more true as the formation of our conscience and is are in harmony with the Cosmic Christ, the Alpha and the Omega.

Pope Francis emphasizes that "the Holy Spirit causes us to contemplate history in the light of the risen Jesus." (#139) [24] He continues with a quote from the New Zealand bishops: "we are capable of loving with the Lord's unconditional love because the risen Lord shares his powerful life with our fragile lives." (#18) [25]

This is why Fr. Al Bischoff is relevant. In his own recognizable life as a priest and pastor of the Catholic Church, as a Jesuit, as a son of Price Hill, he has somehow embodied the truth and the joy of the Risen Christ. It isn't that he is more of a Saint than we are. It's that he knows with conviction that we are all Saints. He lives each day, breathes each breath, with this marvelous Good News. That's why it's called *Good News*; it is the Gospel truth!

The real sacrament of the Risen Christ is in celebrating relationship. This is the crucible in which darkness, self-pity, and cynical resentments are dissolved by love. This is where light, hope, and joy triumph. This is where we participate with Christ in revealing the kingdom, tangibly, intimately, and really. It happens all day, every day, everywhere.

Look for it ... Make it happen ... Enjoy it! Welcome the Reign of God!

CHAPTER 21

The Final Pilgrimage—
The Final Chapter

During Lent of 2020, Al immersed himself in a book that had been given to him as a gift from friends John and Susan Tew. He discovered in *A Pilgrimage to Eternity: From Canterbury to Rome in Search of a Faith* by Timothy Egan a narrative with references surprisingly reminiscent of his own journey.

The starting place of Egan's pilgrimage was the place where all pilgrims who set out on the Via Francigina, "the road that comes from France," begin. There is a one thousand year old tradition to walk this one thousand mile route from Canterbury to Rome as devout Christians followed their lifelong desire to visit the Vatican, the Holy See and the tombs of the apostles, all in search of what they believed to be the source of their faith. The sacred first steps of this pilgrimage begin at the historic death and burial site of Thomas Becket in the Cathedral of Canterbury.

Egan intentionally follows in the footsteps of centuries of seekers. For him the path is not toward a loyal and unquestioning embrace of his family's long faith tradition, but rather a quest in search of reckoning with his own beliefs and truth. Since this traveler does not claim to be a believer, he is a particularly delightful companion for

Al. He has always sought the freshness of the Gospel as it lives in the heart of each person rather than perceiving it as an unexamined orthodoxy uncritically passed on for generations. As his story unfolds, Egan himself describes how he was moved by experiences and conversations with believers along the way.

It turns out that Egan's experience at the grave of St. Thomas is one shared by many pilgrims before him and since, including Al himself. Years ago Al had travelled to Cambridge with his longtime friend Leo Klein, S.J., both of them eager to make the trip from there to Canterbury. When they reached the sacred site of the grave of Thomas Becket, Al was moved to fall to his knees and weep. It was all these years later as he was reading the book that he learned that for centuries pilgrims have been moved in the same way, humbled in the presence of such faith and courage.

As Egan continued the pilgrimage into and through France he learned firsthand the atrocities of the killing of the French Huguenots, made martyrs for their faith through "pogroms" at the hands of imperialistic and brutal Catholics. As Al read these passages he was vividly struck by a memory of an experience when he was campus minister at Augustana years before.

One day when he was walking out on campus and wearing his "Roman collar" he called out to a young man, "Hello Saint" as was his practice. This time, instead of the typical welcomed response, the man ran up to him and aggressively said, "You killed my ancestors, you killed my family!" As Fr. B calmly listened, the young man's anger slowly began to dissipate, and he was eventually able to accept the invitation to pray the Our Father together. The generational bitterness he had carried for so long was transformed by a personal encounter with a Catholic priest. The memory evoked for Al by reading one pilgrim's story all these years later took on a clearer and more stunningly historical context.

This past Lent Al knew that his own humble pilgrimage would be to make his way from the Jesuit residence up the steps shuffling along the path past Brockman Hall slightly uphill to the Chapel each day. His quest has been the gentle sitting before the Eucharist opening his heart to God's tender love with simple rituals now. He awakes at 4:00 AM to spend an hour in the Jesuit residence chapel, then after some rest, has breakfast at 10:00 AM. He then makes his way to the small Eucharistic chapel inside Bellarmine Chapel. The next stop on his daily pilgrimage is what is now called Our Lady of Peace Chapel on campus, beautiful and historic, a gift from the Williams family relocated from their family property in 2017. There in the quiet he rests in his intimate conversations with God.

Al walking to the Chapel as the sun sets in the distance, November 2020.
Courtesy of Mary Anne Reese

Expanding his path he then takes a drive to Eden Park to a favorite place under a grove of trees to pray the rosary, as he says, for "the whole city of Cincinnati." Even there, in the anonymity of a public park, he is reminded of how God continues to reach people through him. He shared that recently a man and his teenage daughter approached him asking to confirm that he was the priest from Xavier who calls people "Saint." They are among the many smitten by the affirmation, and were given this chance encounter to express their gratitude.

As one ages, one's pilgrimage instinctively and necessarily changes. The adventure of travelling thousands of miles in a quest for the grail of a deepening faith or a life decision discerned can be transformed in humility and grace into a return to our original Lover. Now the path is just a few steps to a quiet place of surrender where one opens one's heart to fuller union and Communion with the suffering Jesus and the risen Christ. Al's life has covered both the greatest distances of faith and these more recent small steps that may be the most challenging of all. The blessing of a long life is to finally sit face to face with our original Lover with whom each of us is the beloved.

Al says that the prayer that guides his daily life and stillness more than ever now is the Suscipe given to us by St. Ignatius, essential for every pilgrim at every milestone:

> Take Lord, and receive all my liberty, my memory, my
> understanding, and my entire will, all that I have and possess.
> You have given all to me. To you O lord, I return it. All is
> yours; dispose of it wholly according to your will. Give me
> only your love and your grace. These are enough for me.

This beloved pilgrim did not need to travel the many miles from Canterbury to Rome. Instead, the path he walked was more like the road to Emmaus on which the risen Christ accompanied two discouraged disciples. Their hearts burned within them in the recounting of the Scriptures and the breaking of the bread. In those encounters Al discovered depths in his own faith just as he affirmed true authentic faith in the hearts of so many on the road with him.

Last Words ... How We Will Live, Having Known Fr. B

In an issue of *Religion and Ethics* Rabbi Jonathan Sacks (global religious leader and author) has written, "The Silence of the 'I': Humility as an Unfashionable Virtue."

Humility—true humility—is one of the most expansive and life-enhancing of all virtues. It does not mean undervaluing yourself. It means valuing "other" people. It signals a certain openness to life's grandeur and the willingness to be surprised, uplifted, by goodness wherever one finds it ... The greater part of humility is the capacity to be open to something greater than oneself. False humility is the pretense that one is small. True humility is the consciousness of standing in the presence of greatness, which is why it is the virtue of prophets, those who feel most vividly the nearness of God.

He goes on to describe his experience of meeting the late mystic Rabbi Menachem Mendel Schneerson, considered to be one of the outstanding charismatic leaders of our time. The meeting changed his life.

He was a world-famous figure. I was an anonymous student from three thousand miles away. Yet in his presence I seemed to be the most important person in the world. Quickly it became clear to me that he believed in me more than I believed in myself. As I left the room, it occurred to me that it had been full of my presence and his absence. Perhaps that is what listening is, considered as a religious act. I then knew that greatness is measured by what we efface ourselves towards. There was no grandeur in his manner; neither was there any false modesty. He was serene, dignified, majestic; a man of transcending humility who gathered you into his embrace and taught you to look up.

Humility, then, is more than just a virtue: it is a form of perception, a language in which the "I" is silent so that I can hear the "Thou"—the unspoken call beneath human speech—the Divine whisper within all that moves, the voice of otherness that calls me to redeem its loneliness with the touch of love. Humility is what opens us to the world. [26]

It will be shocking when Fr. B is gone. All of us will be swept back to those encounters with him that we cherish. He would say that he'll be waiting for us to make sure we make it "through the gates." He would say he is still with us. After all, we all believe in "the Communion of Saints, the forgiveness of sins, the Resurrection of the body, and life everlasting."

As friends of Fr. B, we all shared this experience. Each of us is treated as a gift, a treasure. In friendship you never feel confined by him. You are passing through his life and taking something of him with you, but with no obligation. To each of us he says, "Look in the mirror and see the blessed, holy person you are, and be grateful!"

The only real sadness, the only real failure, the only
great tragedy in life is not to have become a Saint.
(French poet Leon Bloy)

The Christian life is "joy in the Holy Spirit." (Rom. 14:17)

No one will take your joy from you. (Jn. 16:22)

What a joy!

Appendix

APPENDIX A: SCRIPTURES ON SAINTS

Fr. B will tell you that this is his favorite passage in all of Scripture is Colossians 3:

Because you are God's chosen ones, holy saints and beloved, clothe yourselves with heartfelt mercy, with kindness, humility, meekness and patience. Bear with one another; forgive whatever grievances you have against one another. Forgive as the Lord has forgiven you. Over all these virtues put on love, which binds the rest together and makes them perfect. Christ's peace must reign in your hearts, since as members of the one body you have been called to that peace. Dedicate yourselves to thankfulness. Let the word of Christ, rich as it is, dwell in you. In wisdom made perfect, instruct and admonish one another. Sing gratefully to God from your hearts in psalms, hymns, and inspired songs. Whatever you do, whether in speech or in action, do it in the name of the Lord Jesus. Give thanks to God the Father through him. (Col. 3: 12–17)

I have come that you may have life and have it abundantly. (Jn.10: 10)

*... that mystery hidden from ages and generations
past but now revealed to his saints.* (Col. 1: 26)

*God will not forget your work and the love you have shown
him by your service, past and present, to his saints. (Other
translation: "serving the saints as you do.")* (Heb. 6: 10)

*He who searches hearts knows what the Spirit means, for the
Spirit intercedes for the saints as God himself wills.* (Rom. 8: 27)

Love the Lord, all you his saints! (Ps. 31: 24)

*To you who have been consecrated in Christ
Jesus and called to be saints ... together with all
those using the name of Jesus.* (I Cor. 1: 2)

*To all in Rome, beloved of God and called to be saints, grace and
peace from God our Father and the Lord Jesus Christ.* Rom. (1: 7)

*By the might of his glory you will be endowed with the
strength needed to stand fast, even to endure joyfully
whatever may come, giving thanks to the Father for having
made you worthy to share the lot of the saints in light.
He rescued us from the power of darkness and brought
us into the kingdom of his Beloved Son.* (Col. 1: 11–13)

*Through him [Christ] we both have access in one Spirit to
the Father. This means that you are strangers and aliens no
longer. No, you are fellow citizens of the saints and members
of the household of God. You form a building which rises on*

the foundation of the apostles and prophets, with Christ Jesus
himself as the capstone. Through him the whole structure
is fitted together and takes shape as a holy temple in the
Lord; in him you are being built into this temple, to become
a dwelling place for God in the Spirit. (Eph. 2: 18–22)

"Saint" (singular) has only one reference in Phil. 4: 21. "Give
my greetings in Christ Jesus to every saint of the church."
There are sixty-seven references to plural "Saints."

APPENDIX B: A CENTURY IN THE LIFE OF THE CHURCH: HOW FR. B GREW WITH HIS CATHOLIC CHURCH

One hundred years of change in the Catholic Church is captured in Al Bischoff's life by theologian Gregory Baum, who died in 2017 at the age of 94. In his *Amazing Church: A Catholic Theologian Remembers a Half-Century of Change,* published in 2005 by Orbis Books, he identifies the extraordinary shifts in the teaching of the Catholic Church in the second half of the twentieth century. Baum knows this very personally, having served as expert for the Second Vatican Council, 1960-1965. In his Preface he writes, "Since we usually emphasize the Church's fidelity to its sacred tradition and sometimes even say that the Church never changes its teaching, the evolution of its official positions on theological and ethical issues over the last fifty years is truly amazing."[27]

In the Spirit-led document *Gaudium et Spes,* the Council dignified our individual conscience as the responsibility and sanctuary of each person to reveal how we are to love God and neighbor. The emerging principles of Catholic social teaching called us to a preferential and imperative choice to live in solidarity with the poor, expressing a new sense of joy and hope of those who seek to be disciples of Christ. We were challenged to embrace the pluralism of God's plan for salvation by opening respectful dialogue with persons of other faiths and to pursue new ecumenical understandings with other Christians.

Here's the part that closely connects with Fr. B's lived spirituality of sainthood. In one of his closing paragraphs Baum writes:

Because the Church's new teaching assigns priority to universal solidarity, it creates a new bond with the Saints, the brothers and sisters who have died in God and now live in the divine light. Since God does not want to be God without us, we do not want to think of God or worship God without acknowledging the bond of solidarity that unites us with the Communion of Saints. [28]

If you have been drawn into Fr. B's way of living, you are embracing the implications of this substantial change in the church even if you have not named them: solidarity with all of humanity, a radical understanding of the Communion of Saints, a sincere hope for all humanity to be saved. He lived out the spirit of Vatican II in moving from conscience to consciousness, realizing that both lead to the same end. For the first two-thirds of his priesthood he sometimes felt his proclamation of the Good News was at odds with the institution. He often felt that he would "get in trouble" by proclaiming the Gospel too generously. During the past few years he has become liberated from this burden. Throughout most of history the church has been scrupulous in defending "truths." At this very moment, Pope Francis himself is showing us that welcoming people as brothers and sisters is often a higher priority than defending orthodoxy.

APPENDIX C: THE EXAMEN

From *A Simple Life-Changing Prayer: Discovering the Power of St. Ignatius Loyola's Examen,* by Jim Manney, Loyola Press 2001:

The Examination of Conscience was the methodical inventory of sins that I was taught to do as a boy ... The charm of this prayer wore off as I grew older. I set it aside ... Then I learned that the Ignatian Examen was *not* the old depressing Examination of Conscience. Quite the opposite. This was a prayer that focused on God's presence in the real world. It looked to a God who was near to me, present in my world, and active in my life. [29]

God is not remote from us. God is at the point of my pen, my pick, my paint brush, my needle—and my heart and my thoughts.
Pierre Teilhard de Chardin, S.J., Hymn of the Universe.

APPENDIX D: *CURA PERSONALIS*

Please read the entire article *"Cura Personalis*: Some Ignatian Inspirations," by Fr. Barton T. Geger, S.J., Jesuit Higher Education 3(2): 6-20 (2014) for more applications of this practice on Jesuit campuses, including:

Care of Faculty and Staff: "Discrete Charity"
Care of Administrators: "The Ignatian Presupposition"
Care of Students: "Spiritual Conversations"

The author develops a few dynamics of spiritual conversations that bear notable connections to other Ignatian themes: contemplation in action, respect for the individual, adaptation or "inculturation," and ends and means. By better grasping how these applications can be lived out in a campus culture, we will all have a better sense of how to continue and insure Fr. B's legacy for the future of all in Jesuit university communities.

APPENDIX E: FR. B'S FAVORITE RECOMMENDED BOOKS AND FILMS

The Contemplative Heart by Jim Finley

The Great Reformer: Francis and the Making of a Radical Pope by Austen Ivereigh

Seven Story Mountain by Thomas Merton

All of Thomas Merton's writings

The Bible and the Holy Writings of Buddhism and Islam

Brideshead Revisited by Evelyn Waugh

The Power and the Glory by Graham Greene

Good Bye, Mr. Chips by James Hilton

The Birds' Christmas Carol by Kate Douglas Wiggin (his mother's favorite book which she read to Al as a child)

St. Francis Xavier 1506-1552 by James Broderick, S.J.

Huckleberry Finn & Tom Sawyer by Mark Twain

A Tale of Two Cities by Charles Dickens

Gone With the Wind by Margaret Mitchell (Al read this book in the 8th grade and got in trouble with the nuns; although it romanticized war, he loved stories of the South)

All Quiet on the Western Front by Erich Maria Remarque (insights into war)

The Rise and Fall of the Third Reich by William L. Shirer (insights into war)

To Kill a Mockingbird by Harper Lee (insights into racism)

Revelation by Flannery O'Connor

A Pilgrimage to Eternity: From Canterbury to Rome in Search of a Faith by Timothy Egan

Lives of the Saints & biographies of famous people

Favorite plays

The Glass Menagerie and others by Tennessee Williams

Death of a Salesman and others by Arthur Miller

Plays by William Shakespeare

Enjoyed season tickets to The Ensemble Theater with Leo Klein
for many years

Musicals

Oklahoma

South Pacific

Carousel

Les Miserables

Miss Saigon

Favorite films

Gone with the Wind

The Wizard of Oz

Remains of the Day

The King's Speech

Schindler's List

The Shawshank Redemption

Alfred Hitchcock films

Italian art films made in the '60s

Book List for further reading

(in addition to those in endnotes below)

*Spiritual Intimacy and Community: An Ignatian view of the Small
Faith Community* by John English, S.J.

Consolations by David Whyte

River Flow by David Whyte

Silence on Fire by William Shannon

Dining in the Kingdom of God by Eugene LaVerdiere

A Simple Life-Changing Prayer: Discovering the Power of St. Ignatius Loyola's Examen by Jim Manney

Inner Compass by Margaret Silf

The Ignatian Adventure by Kevin O'Brien

The Soul of a Pilgrim by Christine Valters Painter

My Life with the Saints by James Martin, S.J.

Ordinary People as Monks and Mystics by Marcia Sinetar

Merton's Palace of Nowhere by Jim Finley

The Guardian of Mercy by Terence Ward

God's Voice Within by Mark Thibodeaux, S.J.

Immortal Diamond by Richard Rohr

Given for You: Reflections on the Meaning of the Lord's Supper by Louis Accola

Intimacy with God by Thomas Keating

New Seeds of Contemplation by Thomas Merton

Amazing Church: A Catholic Theologian Remembers a Half-Century of Change by Gregory Baum

Mercy: The Essence of the Gospel and the Key to Christian Life by Cardinal Walter Kasper, translated by William Madges

Sacred Fire by Ronald Rohlheiser

APPENDIX F: FR. B'S HOMILY TO GRADUATES MAY 2020

Well, let me begin by wishing all of your mothers a blessed and a Happy Mother's Day. One might think that a conflict exists between Mother's Day and a Mass to celebrate one's graduation from college. Not so. Your parents had a dream. You, Saints, are that dream. Your father probably initiated the process but your mother brought that dream to life. So honor your mother today and remember to honor your father on his day in June.

The Gospel begins with these words, "Do not let your hearts be troubled." As your parents had a dream, you also came to Xavier with the dream of one day gathering in the Cintas Center and graduating this coming week. That dream will not happen.

Let me tell you a story.

Way back in another century, I graduated from this university from that old fieldhouse on the other side of campus. As I left the stage and walked out of that building I only remember one thing. Tears rolled down my cheek. I have no memory of who talked, who got the awards or anything. I only remember the tears. Those tears indicated that I was sad. Something wonderful had happened during the past four years that I could never again experience.

My grandmother taught me as a little boy that it is alright to cry. You can let go of the source of the tears and get a clearer vision. A clearer vision showed me that I had my degree, the friends I had made, the teachers who believed in me, the memory of wonderful weekends of fun and sports events. Really, I had lost nothing, but my dream had not come to completion as I had imagined.

But the real dream was to live in the moment—one day at a time. The past is yesterday; the future is tomorrow. You will experience fear at times, but you do not have to live in fear. Occasionally, you might make poor choices. We all do. Simply name and claim these poor choices. Do not run from them. Your life will become stronger. You will have clearer vision with courage to begin again. Yes, times of doubt will haunt you. Listen to the doubt. Doubt can stimulate new ways of thinking and draw you to a deeper understanding of truth. Reflect on the experiences of your life. Learn from your mistakes and give thanks. Then you will live a life filled with hope and promise.

Remember, the world you are entering is not easy; not a Graeter's ice cream cone or a Saturday night beer at Dana's. It is a tough world but it is God's world and God calls you to take your faith and your education with you along with your family values and your dream. Believe in that dream and in yourself. Begin there. Your parents believe in you or you would not be breathing here. Your professors believe in you or you would not be getting a degree. Your friends believe in you or you would not have such fantastic friends. Fr. Graham believes in you and I believe in you. You are our Saints. And finally, God believes in you!

Listen again to the Gospel. Jesus is going home to prepare a place for you. And never forget that you became one in Jesus Christ because Sunday after Sunday you came together at the 4:00 or 10:00 PM Mass and heard an invitation to become his Body. You heard stories from him that enabled you to understand yourself, showing you how to live in our beautiful and broken world. And before you left, Christ fed you with his bread that is more than bread, with wine that is more than wine. He fed you his Body and Blood, so that day after day He would be one with you, his presence, his life and his truth. He fed you, quite frankly, so that you could become his love, the only love that will heal his broken world.

Today's Gospel reminds us that Philip and Thomas did doubt and did fear as they gathered on Easter night. But Jesus entered. You will find in your life, as I have found in my own life, Saints, that Jesus the Christ still walks through locked doors. "Fear not! I am with you!"

XAVIER
UNIVERSITY

The Dorothy Day Center for Faith and Justice
3800 Victory Parkway
Cincinnati, Ohio 45207-2141
www.xavier.edu/cfj

November 1, 2018

Archbishop Dennis M. Schnurr
Archdiocese of Cincinnati
100 East 8th Street
Cincinnati, Ohio 45202

My Archbishop Dennis,

    I read your letter to the priests concerning the Bishops as a body spending a week in prayer and fasting in reparation for the mishandling of child abuse by church ministers. I want to thank you and the Bishops for this action. I am myself a victim.

    At an early age, I was sexually abused by a relative and a priest of the Archdiocese of Cincinnati. I first discovered this as I was praying before the Blessed Sacrament while living in Rock Island, Illinois. The image of one of the abusers came before the Tabernacle. I cried out, "How could you do this to me?" With the support of my Jesuit companions, I was able to go into therapy for ten years with the late Dr. Richard Brush. Quite frankly, without this insightful care and concern, I do not think that I would be living today. Three of those years I would have sessions 2 or 3 times a week. I am a blessed man as I discovered a loving God and the fear, doubt, sexual confusion and, at times, a sense of worthlessness in which I lived most of my life, grace has and is healing me. I can only give deep thanks that I did not abuse anyone. My life has been a blessing for others because God has given me a most compassionate heart and a patiently, listening ear. Many people come to me that are turned away by others. I myself was told to leave the Confessional because I was not a good man. The priest did give me Absolution. (He was not a priest of the Archdiocese.)

    My writing this letter comes from much prayer using the Spiritual Exercises of Saint Ignatius. I am not angry anymore and have forgiven those who have done this to me. I ask nothing from the Archdiocese and I feel and have always felt blessed to minister in this Archdiocese. I shall join with you and the Bishops in your days of fasting and prayer. Thank God we have a Father of love and forgiveness, a God who loves us more when we are hurting the most, not a God who lives by rules but offers mercy and understanding.

Sincerely,

Albert Bischoff, S.J.

Albert Bischoff, S.J.

Cc: Bishop Joseph Binzer

163

Office of
The Archbishop

100 East Eighth Street
Cincinnati, Ohio 45202

513-421-3131 Ext. 2810

November 5, 2018

PERSONAL & CONFIDENTIAL

Reverend Albert Bischoff, S.J.
Xavier University
The Dorothy Day Center for Faith and Justice
3800 Victory Parkway
Cincinnati, Ohio 45207-2141

Dear Father Bischoff,

Thank you for your recent letter. I apologize for the abuse that you suffered due to the actions of one of our priests some years ago. I am also grateful to your Jesuit community which has been such a support to you personally. Please be assured of my prayers.

Also thank you for joining Bishop Binzer and me in extra prayer and fasting in the days leading up to the General Assembly of Bishops next week. We need to review and create policies but, perhaps more importantly, we need to pray for spiritual renewal.

With prayers and best wishes, I am

Sincerely yours in Christ,

Most Reverend Dennis M. Schnurr
Archbishop of Cincinnati

lsc
cc: Bishop Joseph Binzer

This letter is reproduced with the permission of the author.

Endnotes

1   Pope Francis, *Gaudete et Exsultate: On the Call to Holiness in Today's World* (Vatican City: Libreria Editrice Vaticana, 2018), #1

2   Pope Francis, *Gaudete et Exsultate: On the Call to Holiness in Today's World* (Vatican City: Libreria Editrice Vaticana, 2018), #138

3   *The Order of Baptism of Children,* (English translation), (Washington: USCCB Committee on Divine Worship, 2017.)

4   Adapted from Richard Rohr, *True Self/ False Self* (Franciscan Media: 2003, 2013), disc 1 and handout (CD); and *Immortal Diamond: The Search for Our True Self* (Jossey-Bass: 2013), 17. Thomas Merton, *Conjectures of a Guilty Bystander* (Image Books: 1968), 156.

5   Richard Rohr, Center for Action and Contemplation. *True Self/ False Self Week 1: A Point of Nothingness* 08–05–2016.

6   Adapted from Richard Rohr, *True Self/ False Self* (Franciscan Media: 2003, 2013), disc 1 (CD); and *Immortal Diamond: The Search for Our True Self* (Jossey-Bass: 2013).

7   Jay Earley, *Self-Therapy: A Step-By-Step Guide to Creating Wholeness and Healing Your Inner Child Using IFS, A New Cutting-Edge Psychotherapy,* (Minneapolis: Mill City Press, 2009), Foreword, x, xi.

8   Thomas Merton, *New Seeds of Contemplation* (Boulder: Shambhala, 2003), 36.

9   Adapted from Richard Rohr, *True Self/ False Self* (Franciscan Media: 2003, 2013), disc 1 (CD); and *Immortal Diamond: The Search for Our True Self* (Jossey-Bass: 2013)

10 Margaret Silf, *Companions of Christ: Ignatian Spirituality for Everyday Living,* (Grand Rapids: Eerdmans Publishing Co., 2004), 8–9.

11 Pope Francis, *Gaudete et Exsultate: On the Call to Holiness in Today's World* (Vatican City: Libreria Editrice Vaticana, 2018) #22.

12 Center for Action and Contemplation, "You are the 'Imago Dei'" Richard Rohr, OFM, July 31, 2016.

13 Center for Action and Contemplation, "In God's Eyes" Richard Rohr, OFM, August 4, 2016.

14 Adapted from Richard Rohr, "He Looks Just Like Everybody Else!" Homily given at Holy Family Catholic Church, Albuquerque, NM, on April 10, 2016, https://cac.org/looks-just-like-everybody-else/; and *Immortal Diamond: The Search for Our True Self* (Jossey-Bass: 2013), 181–183. Richard's Daily Meditations, December 30, 2017. https://cac.org/from-the-bottom-up-summary-weekly-summary-2017-12-30/.

15 Adapted from Richard Rohr, *True Self/ False Self* (Franciscan Media: 2003, 2013), disc 1 and handout (CD); and *Immortal Diamond: The Search for Our True Self* (Jossey-Bass: 2013), 17.

16 Fr. Barton T. Geger, S.J., "*Cura Personalis*: Some Ignatian Inspirations," Jesuit Higher Education 3(2): 6–20 (2014)

17 *Catechism of the Catholic Church,* (Rome: Libreria Editrice Vaticana, 1994), #1326.

18 Pope Francis, *Gaudete et Exsultate: On the Call to Holiness in Today's World* (Vatican City: Libreria Editrice Vaticana, 2018), #147.

19 Pope Francis, *Gaudete et Exsultate: On the Call to Holiness in Today's World* (Vatican City: Libreria Editrice Vaticana, 2018) #149.

20 "Communion of saints tapestries," September, 2002, http://www.olacathedral.org/cathedral/art/tapestries.html

21 Pope Francis, *Gaudete et Exsultate: On the Call to Holiness in Today's World* (Vatican City: Libreria Editrice Vaticana, 2018) #19–21.

22 Pope Francis, *Gaudete et Exsultate: On the Call to Holiness in Today's World* (Vatican City: Libreria Editrice Vaticana, 2018) #109.

23 Isabelle R. Moyer, *"Proud to be a Cafeteria Catholic,"* Parish Life, (July 21, 2015.)

24 Pope Francis, *Gaudete et Exsultate: On the Call to Holiness in Today's World* (Vatican City: Libreria Editrice Vaticana, 2018) #139.

25 Pope Francis, *Gaudete et Exsultate: On the Call to Holiness in Today's World* (Vatican City: Libreria Editrice Vaticana, 2018) #18.

26 Rabbi Jonathan Sacks, "The Silence of the 'I': Humility as an Unfashionable Virtue," *Religion and Ethics,* (June, 2018.)

27 Gregory Baum, *Amazing Church: A Catholic Theologian Remembers a Half-Century of Change* (Maryknoll: Orbis Books, 2005), Preface, 135.

28 Gregory Baum, *Amazing Church: A Catholic Theologian Remembers a Half-Century of Change* (Maryknoll: Orbis Books, 2005), 150.

29 Jim Manney, *A Simple Life-Changing Prayer: Discovering the Power of St. Ignatius Loyola's Examen*, (Chicago: Loyola Press, 2011), preface.